THE 6-STEP PLAN

RISING TO GREATNESS TO FULFILL YOUR DESTINY

BY

LAUREN C. WARD

LIFE TO LEGACY, LLC

The 6-Step Plan: Rising to Greatness to Fulfill Your Destiny

By: Lauren C. Ward

ISBN 13: 978-1-939654-33-5
IBSN 10: 1939654335

Printed in the United States
10 9 8 7 6 5 4 3 2 1

Cover concept by: Lauren C. Ward

Cover design by: Tasha Sykes
                  Legacy Designs, Inc.
                  Legacydesigninc@gmail.com

Published by:
Life To Legacy, LLC
2441 Vermont Street, #57
Blue Island, IL 60406
(877) 267-7477
www.Life2Legacy.com

Presented To:

Contact the author at:
Lward98@gmail.com

CONTENTS

Dedication   6

Acknowledgements   7

1.   God First   9

2.   Education   27

3.   Career   43

4.   Your Own Place   89

5.   Marriage   101

6.   Kids   113

7.   The Journey Continues   127

DEDICATION

This book is dedicated to my astonishing and beautiful parents Marilyn and Yogi Ward. They are an irreplaceable canvas that will always rank number one in my life.

I also dedicate this book to my students because the bond I share with them is beyond special. Words cannot express how special you are to me.

ACKNOWLEDGEMENTS

I would like to first and foremost thank my parents Marilyn and Yogi Ward for giving me the support, guidance, and motivation to write my first book. They have been by my side since the beginning and they will always be my guardian angels. I want to thank my grandma Johnnie Mae Greer, my aunties Marsha Greer, Lauren Greer, Lynn Napoleon and Mary Farrell, my uncles John Ward, and Victor Ward, and my cousins Tiffany, Rasheed, Bernadette, Natasha, Jalen, Karolina, Maryah, Ravan, Reaell, Marshona, Skye, and Skylar for always believing in me. I especially want to thank my cousins who feel more like my siblings. My older sister Ashley Shambley, my younger sister Brittany Jett and my little brother Brandon Redmond for loving me endlessly and being the rocks in my life I can always count on. I would like to thank my late grandparents Victor Ward and Mary Ward for their continuous love and support.

I want to thank my devoted and loving boyfriend of five years Tyshaun Martin "Ty" for always being my better half and my total support system. I want to thank my mentor Cheryl Burton, Evelyn Holmes, Dr. Winston Johnson, Sharon Houston-Culbreath and Pastor Rev. Derrick B Wells. I also want to thank Dr. Dennis and Chantia Woods for their continued faith that I would complete this book even when I didn't know how I would pull it off. All I can say is that I am grateful and blessed God placed a power couple like them in my circle because what they have done for me will never be forgotten.

My deepest appreciation to a host of family, grandparents, friends, colleagues, sorors, prophytes, line sisters, fraternity brothers, hair stylists, extended family and complete strangers who have given me their wisdom, support, and unconditional love to encourage me to write this book and follow my dreams.

Chapter One

God First

Before I begin, I want you to know that this book was created for teenagers, young adults, and adults. If you don't know what to do after high school, or college, and you need guidance these steps will help you to be successful in life.

I was born on December 25th, 1988 at 9:38 p.m. I was brought home in a Christmas stocking and given a bible! Who knew that my unconditional love and my spiritual beliefs would be formed so early by my family from birth? I was always taught to put God first. I was told if you ever have a problem, call on God because he's the one that will never leave nor forsake you.

I grew up in church. I remember being baptized at St. Margaret of Scotland and attending bible study classes. I remember hearing Reverend Dr. Johnnie Coleman speak at Christ Universal Temple.

Johnnie Coleman said, "It works if you work it." It was then that I decided at a young age that I needed help going through this journey called life. I tried to talk to everyone about my problems but I realized becoming one with God and understanding the concept of "peace be still" was the medicine I needed if I was going to heal.

The first step to feeling unconditional love and being successful, prosperous, happy, fruitful, and peaceful is putting Jesus Christ first in your life. He's your everything! When things aren't going right in your life, ask yourself when was the last time you prayed to God, read the bible, gone to church, or even meditated to connect with God spiritually?

Being spiritually connected to God is so important in order to achieve your dreams. Once you accept Christ into your life, there's no way you can't be successful. My grandma Johnnie Mae would always walk me to church. She constantly reminded me that the Lord loved me. My grandma is ninety years old. I love her dearly for taking me under her wing, and loving me like the Lord loves us. My mom and aunties are blessed to have her as a mom because she is truly an angel. My grandma is the one who told me that you start an excellent relationship with God by honoring him. You need to worship God every day and praise his name when you feel doubtful about any situation you're going through. When you wake up in the morning, acknowledge him by simply saying, "Thank you, God."

It is crucial that you remember to thank God for everything, especially the smaller things in life that so many of us take for granted. It's a blessing to have a roof over your head, food to eat, and clothes on your back. Some people are homeless and don't know when their next meal is coming. They're searching for old clothes in garbage cans. Even being able to breathe is a blessing. Someone is fighting for their life in a hospital, depending on an oxygen tank to survive. That's why I say we can't be so busy that we don't have time for God. We have to make time for him! When my grandma on my dad's side of the family passed away I was heartbroken but then I had to remember the relationship my grandmother had with the Lord. I had to remember the relationship I have with the Lord and that's when I became content because to live to the age of 97 is a blessing! God made it possible for her to live that long so instead of complaining I was thankful for that.

Louise L. Hay said, "I find the more willing I am to be grateful for the small things in life, the bigger stuff just seems to show up from unexpected sources, and I am constantly looking forward to each day with all the surprises that keep coming my way."

In other words, take time to smell the roses and enjoy the smaller things in life that you may not have noticed before. Are you really good at painting? Are you a really good singer or writer? Are you an excellent test taker? These are talents and gifts that were given to you that not everyone can do. Be thankful for them. Everyone can't be Beyoncé, J.K. Rowling, or Vincent Van Gogh. The reason is because you're an original, not a copy! Something that comes easy to you doesn't necessarily come easy for someone else, so appreciate the smaller things in life!

If you receive an A on an exam, take time and thank God. If you were blessed with a new job, take time and thank God. If you see, smell, touch, feel, and hear, please take time and thank God. As much as you watch TV, listen to music, attend parties, and travel, you need to take time out of your day so that you can thank God.

Once you understand what your priorities are and you make a list of what your values need to be, your life will begin to take a turn down a better road. For example, my priorities in life are my family, respecting myself, knowing my self-worth, being at peace, being happy, having genuine friends in my circle, and not caring what others think about me.

My values are having God first in my life, having an education, maintaining a successful career in a field I'm passionate about, having my own place, being married and having children. Well what do you know my values are my 6-step plan! At this time I want you to get out a pen, a notebook or a sheet of paper because these are the bullet points I want you to write down!

- God First
- Education
- Career
- Your Own Place
- Marriage
- Kids

My values and priorities are what ground me. My 6-step plan is what I live for! My plan motivates me to work harder and it allows me to have an ambitious mindset. I have grown so much spiritually, emotionally, physically, and consciously because of my 6-step plan. I am the thinker that can believe in my dreams, set goals and tear down any boundaries. As the saying goes, if you don't stand for something, you will fall for anything. So what are you going to stand for? What will your values and priorities be? Will you dream big or small? Will you set goals or be afraid to because you have put in your conscience that you will fail? Don't bury your dreams let your dreams live and you can get there by following my 6-step plan. Young people, that's why it's so important to know who and whose you are. Once you know who and whose you are, baby, you can conquer the world. Don't let anyone tell you differently!

You're the child of a king. God made no mistakes when he created you. Have faith in yourself, have faith in God, and have faith that you will make it. Second Chronicles chapter 15 verse 7 says, "But as for you be strong and do not give up for your work will be rewarded."

So understand that nothing you do is a waste of time. It's setting you up for where you're supposed to be. Greater is coming for you. Sometimes you have to go around to the back door or through a side window just to get through the front door.

Take me for example. I've been fighting for a job in my field for two-and-a-half years! I graduated from Howard University in 2011 with my B.A. in Broadcast Journalism. In 2012, I graduated from Northwestern University with my M.S. in Communications. You couldn't have told me that I was going to be working at Victoria's Secret, or as a substitute teacher. But you know what? It took those experiences to make me into the strong black woman I am today. This whole time, I was thinking why is God doing this? Doesn't he know that I was supposed to graduate with my Masters, land a job on air as a reporter, and start making a lot of money?

God knew what MY plan was, but my plan didn't align with his plan. God knew that I had been doing motivational speaking since the age of thirteen and he knew that I had a greater purpose. God has always wanted me to be involved with the youth. It took me two years to figure that out. God placed me in positions that I didn't want in order to show me my gift.

It started at Victoria's Secret. At first, I was excited

about the job but I kept saying in my head, "This is just temporary. I won't be here long." It wasn't long before I hated the job but I kept telling myself, "You need the money, so you need to do something to make your experience here worthwhile." What did I do? I started talking to all my co-workers. I didn't want to only get to know the co-workers in my department. I wanted to get to know the co-workers in all the departments.

They started opening up to me about their personal lives and before I knew it, the word was going around that I had inspired several people at my job. It was such an amazing feeling! I told one girl who is a single mom about my idea for my book and my 6-step plan. She asked me if she could write it down. She said that when her two-year-old daughter became old enough, she wanted to share the 6-step plan with her.

Right then and there, that humbled me. It made me feel powerful and it made me emotional because I didn't know that she valued my idea that much. People started asking me why I even worked at Victoria's Secrets. They told me I should quit and solely focus on motivational speaking. But of course I didn't because I needed the money. I wasn't ready to step out on faith just yet. Not until I started seeing how much I impacted everyone at my job.

After I was there for two years, I told myself it was time to move on. That's how I started substitute teaching. God placed me where he needed me. Using me as his messenger, he made sure I affected everyone, as a fearless leader should. If you didn't know, God has already given you spiritual genes just like the genes you share from your parents. Your heavenly father has already given you the skill set that's needed; so don't be complacent with mediocrity. Even though you can't see what God has in store for you, just keep the faith. I promise you he has a plan that will manifest when it's your time. It's normal to doubt yourself. I know I definitely did a few times but don't allow that mindset to dictate your future. T. D. Jakes said, "It takes courage to be different." So don't be afraid to be who you are.

I remember when I was a sophomore in college, I had a breakdown because I just couldn't figure myself out. I realize now it was just because I didn't want to accept my assignment from the Lord. But thank God for my mom because she helped me get right back on track. I called her on the phone crying and she could've just brought me home from school but instead she was able to calm me, by praying with me and uplifting me. She told me over and over again that there was nothing wrong with me. She told me later on when she got off the phone, she broke down crying and praying that God would protect me and help me to realize that I'm special.

In 2014, I asked my mom why she stares at me. She said, "Because I thank God for blessing me with you. Every time I look at you, I'm reminded of how wonderful you are. Every time I encounter someone, they tell me how beautiful your spirit is and how wonderful you are! I see you every day, so I already know how wonderful you are. But when someone else says it, I'm reminded of how special you really are."

She then brought up the 2008 incident when I called her from school crying. She said, "I remember asking myself, "Why does my child think there's something wrong with her?" I want her to know there's nothing wrong with her. But now, I'm happy you questioned if there was something wrong with you, Lauren, because now you know that you're different. You touch people's lives, my Lauren Christina, and that is a gift that God blessed you with at an early age! He put it right in front of your face and if you don't use it, you're crazy baby!"

From my mom reminding me of that moment and explaining why she stares at me, I received the encouragement I needed to keep pushing. I was no longer afraid to be different.

I even remember the night I slept in between my parents in their bed. I was distraught that night because someone had stolen my phone. I was out with friends at a party that evening and I was extremely tired. I fell asleep on the couch and when I woke up my phone was gone. I was devastated because I wasn't bringing in any income and I was tired of my parents taking care of me. I knew me and my parents were struggling, so I thought to myself, "How are we going to afford to get me a new phone?" My parents practically already paid all my bills, so I felt bad that I was going to be adding on another expense. I was so angry, I couldn't stop crying.

My parents had to literally calm me down, rub my head and sing me to sleep that night. When I woke up the next day, I was right next to my mom and dad. Of course, I felt like a little baby, but it's moments like this that I will always cherish.

When I hit rock bottom my parents were there for me and they didn't judge me. They loved me unconditionally. They accepted my mistake and the next day they came up with a solution on how we were going to move forward with purchasing a new phone.

Right then and there, I just thanked God for blessing me with the most amazing parents in the world. My dad said, "Lauren, you're better than good. You're great. So don't allow anyone to intervene in your space. Block out all the haters and don't allow anything or anyone that isn't greatness to occupy your space! How dare you allow someone to define your greatness? You know you're better than that. Stop trying to make friends, and recognize your parents and family that have always been there. I was born in 1944, your mom was born in 1955 and you were born in 1988. We were all born in the year of double digit numbers so when you get discouraged remind yourself of the history that runs throughout your veins. Your momma and me have always been a part of you even before you were born. That's why I say 44, 55, and 88." I said, "Wow daddy I didn't know that." He reminded me that he and my mom have always been my biggest cheerleaders and supporters since day one. He reminded me that he and my mom had never missed a motivational speech, a fashion show, a school play, a graduation, a dinner dance, a prom, a ballet recital, a bill, a probate, a baptism, a birthday party, or my first steps.

He said, "It's time for you to take control of your life. Get back that drive that kept you pushing ahead at Howard when you almost didn't graduate on time because of one math class, senior year. It's time for you to get that drive back that you had when you didn't even get into Howard because your application was late. But you kept calling Howard everyday and emailing them until Mrs. House answered the phone to tell you that you have been accepted. It's time for you to get that drive back that propelled you forward when you didn't get into AKA or Phi Sigma Pi the first time. Wake up, girl. Be the strong, intelligent, independent, aggressive, and unique young woman I raised you to be. You already proved you have it in you so activate the strength that God has instilled within you.

Remember that you are a Ward and when you take the d off that means War so go to work boo boo."

As I was sitting there crying, he lifted up my chin and said, "Lauren, I told you to listen to the still small voice from God. You're greater than good boo boo! If you keep working hard or grinding like you young people say you'll have every dream answered that you ever prayed for." I fell into my dad's arms and I just couldn't stop thanking him because I needed him to be hard on me. I needed him to remind me of the strength that lies deep within. That's when I thought back to the day I spoke with Mrs. House. On the phone I told her to accept me into her institution because I would be the one to make a difference. I would be the one to leave behind a legacy. I eat, breathe and sleep Howard University. Thinking about what I said that day made me proud! There have been so many people along my journey that have tried to break me down because I'm a gentle spirit with a kind heart. But the reason their tactics always fail is because of my mom, dad, and God.

My parents are always there to lift me up. As long as I have them in my corner, I can't fail. I'm like an energizer bunny, with my parents as my batteries. I'm just going to keep going and going! My enemy can knock me down, but trust me, I will always get back up and I will be stronger than before. My friend Kea told me a few days later, "Lauren, I just want you to remember to pray. When you get down and out, just remember that your greater is coming, babe!" Now I always keep in mind that my greater is coming. With that mindset, there's no way I can't prosper abundantly.

If you really want to repay God, then repay him through prayer. Repay him by following his assignment he gave to you. Nobody is perfect, so if you have a moment where someone or something takes you to a negative place, pray about it. If you allow yourself to get angry, then take that energy and work even harder on achieving your dream. It's okay to be vulnerable sometimes. It's okay to admit something or someone really upset you that day. It's okay to be afraid at first but the only person that will be able to restore your energy and make you whole again is God.

Give all your negative energy to God. Trust me; he will give you back the positive energy that you need to move forward. Reverend Wells is another spiritual leader that I admire at my church. He said, "You have to decide what you want and what is keeping you from it. If you say you want to be prosperous but you keep speaking into existence how broke you are, then your outcome will never be different."

If you keep saying you want a healthy relationship but you continue to stay in a relationship that is broken, you will never be happy. Allow yourself to open up your heart to God so that you can receive your blessings. You're the only one standing in the way of them. Let me tell you about another situation where I discovered I was standing in my own way.

In 2014 I kept stating how I wanted to be a well-known speaker, how I want to have a lot of money, and how I want to be working in my career field as a reporter. I never thought in a million years that all along, God had been setting up exactly what I wanted. I didn't know that God had not only planned on me being a speaker but maybe even a minister.

In 2014, I met a beautiful, good-hearted woman who is a realtor. She asked me if I was an Evangelist. At the time, I didn't know what an Evangelist was. I chuckled and said, "No, I'm a Christian."

She said, "I know that, sweetie."

And I said, "Ohhhh ... well ... yes ... I do motivational speaking."

I figured that an Evangelist had to pertain to speaking because usually people always say they can tell I'm a speaker. She said, "I could tell because of your voice and your presence." I thought to myself, "Wow, Lauren. You really are supposed to be a motivational speaker, inspiring people everywhere." I was thinking that I was just going to be in the community doing the motivational speaking. But after that experience, she made me think about traveling the world as an Evangelist. I would not only be a motivational speaker, but I could discuss the word of God in different countries.

Here I was blocking my blessing and thinking inside a box. But this woman allowed me to think outside of the box. She took my dream and put it on a bigger spectrum for me to see the whole canvas. I knew at that moment that God had given her that message to deliver to me. So now the question was what was I going to do with the information? I decided to read the bible more, I attended church more and I spoke to God about this life altering decision. I said God, "Please come into my life and order my steps. Allow me to accept your will Lord and help me to trust in your plan. Anything or anyone that does not add to my life please remove it so that I can fully accept my assignment from you oh Lord."

The reason I prayed this prayer is because sometimes you have to learn how to activate and deactivate things in your life. Deactivate "I'm broke." Deactivate "This family member wasn't successful so I won't be either." Deactivate "I think I'll be successful but I'm not sure." Activate "I am somebody." Activate "I will be successful." Activate "I will get a job in my field." Activate "Nobody can stop me, even on my worst day." You can become your own worst critic, but once you learn how to activate positivity in your life and deactivate negativity, you will be much happier. I challenge you to talk to God about everything that's going right in your life and talk to him about things that are bothering you too. You don't have to hold your feelings inside. Get them off your chest, and once you do, just move forward and don't dwell on the past. Let go of all baggage so you can fulfill the assignment God has given to you!

This next piece of advice is for young people and adults. Don't tell everyone your business or put it on social media. Everyone may not understand what you're struggling with, and when people judge your situation or your assignment from God it can be hurtful. That's why I said God is the best solution to help you with your issues. He can give you the closure that you need. Yes, it's okay to open up to a parent or a best friend, but make sure if you're letting a human being in your circle, he or she can be trusted. A wise man who I call my father once told me that not everyone deserves a front row seat in your life. I believe that wholeheartedly because everyone can't make the cut to be your "best friend."

Choose your friends wisely and you can start by making God number one. My Auntie Chubby and my Auntie Lynn are truly my rocks because whenever I felt like I needed friends, they always reminded me that they were my friends. Auntie Chubby would say, "Well you know, Christina, you've always been my namesake so I'm all you need." Then my Auntie Lynn would say, "Well you know,

Lauren Chris, you look like my twin anyway so the only real friend you need is me." I just sat back and laughed because God really blessed me with an amazing family. My family is very small but we're all really close. I can't thank God enough for placing genuine, loving, supportive, and phenomenal people in my life.

My Auntie Marsha is also a person I admire because she was the first African American woman to be a flight attendant for Continental Airlines. She opened up a door for African Americans. I want to strive to continue that legacy. Whether that is through speaking, journalism, teaching, or ministry, I want to open up doors for minorities as well.

For this exercise you can use your notebook or the same sheet of paper you began writing your 6-step plan on. Ask yourself how is my relationship with God? How can I make the connection stronger? How is my family's relationship with God? I want you to answer these questions and then I want you to list what you do to praise God. Once you have completed this task, reflect on what you wrote and evaluate yourself on whether you have given God enough time or if you need to take more time to commit your life to him.

Chapter Two

Education

⚯

Nelson Mandela said, "Education is the most powerful weapon that we can use to change the world." Having an education truly is the gateway to freedom. Anyone can take away your house, your children, the clothes off your back, or even a job. But your education is something no one can ever take away from you. From the moment I stepped foot into elementary school, my parents had already stressed the importance of an education.

My parents entered me into spelling bees, did my homework with me, met my teachers, made sure I respected my teachers, allowed me to stay late to get extra help with my homework, and made sure that my grades were nothing less than a B! I knew at an early age what achieving excellence meant. I strived to do it every day. Even when I made a mistake by bringing home a grade lower than a

B, I never let that discourage me. I was always honest with my parents. I accepted what I did wrong and continued to move forward by excelling the next semester.

Young people, I don't care how horrible it may seem, always be honest with your parents or the person that is taking care of you. They can get you the help you need. If you need a tutor or if you need to take summer classes, do it because it will benefit you in the long run. Don't be embarrassed if you don't understand a subject matter; just ask for help. I was terrible in math and you know what I did? I asked for help because I wasn't going to let that obstacle hold me back. I wasn't going to let math define me. I defined it. I still remember taking math classes over the summer so I could excel in high school as well as college.

Attending elementary school at St. Margaret of Scotland and Marya Yates really helped me realize how valuable an education was. Since my parents had already instilled the values of having an education within me, I surrounded myself with students who had the same mindset as me. That's why I took the extra classes over the summer because I knew it would enhance my knowledge and prepare me for the future. Eleanor Roosevelt said, "Great minds discuss ideas; average minds discuss events; and small minds discuss people." Ask yourself what type of mindset do you have? I realized that I am always discussing ideas, which reassures me that I have a great mind and that I have a great circle. So make sure you are associating with the right people because if your circle of friends is gossiping more than discussing how to get ahead you may want to do some rearranging with your friends.

My mom and dad were both raised in a poor urban area in Chicago so they didn't have much. They went from having nothing to being successful. I yearned for that. My mom has her bachelor's degree and two masters. My dad wasn't able to finish college because he was drafted to the Army, but in the short amount of time that he was at Kennedy King College, he acted and gained entrepreneurship skills. My mom and dad were always discussing ideas. Remember, the quote I just mentioned states how great minds are always discussing how to get ahead and that's exactly what they did. They had great mindsets, which led to success.

After the service, my dad started his own transportation business when he was only twenty-two. We lived in a nice house. There was always food on the table, I always had nice clothes, and for the most part I didn't have any worries. That's why I knew that I wanted to have that same life when I grew up. I thought to myself, "If you can get all of this from having an education, then sign me up!" I knew that the fastest way I could obtain a nice house, money, nice clothes, and anything else I desired was by having an education. I'm very passionate about having an education. That's why I was determined to obtain my bachelor's degree, master's degree, and Ph.D. I have my bachelor's and my master's. The next step on my list is to obtain my Ph.D.

I know some people disagree with going to school because they feel that it costs too much, it takes up to much time, or it is simply a waste of time. But I look at it like this: what else are you going to do? I tell people all the time, especially my students in high school, if you're worried about money, apply for scholarships and look into financial aid or loans. There are definitely ways that you can pay for college. And trust me; college is not an experience you want to miss. The majority of the people I know attended college. The few friends I know that didn't go regret it. They tried to get a job or get in their career without an education and now they have to go back to school.

I'm telling you young people there's a process for everything. There's no career you can obtain overnight. If you want to be a construction worker, doctor, police officer, fire fighter, reporter, or a beautician you will be required to have a degree, license, or certification.

I know some people who are non-traditional students, meaning they're over thirty and realized they should go back to school. Nine times out of ten, it's harder at that age to go back to school because you might have children, or a full time job that won't permit you to take time off of work for school. The best time to attend college is right after high school. Don't' take a break! Sometimes when you take a break it's harder to go back to school and you begin to procrastinate. Also, if you have the opportunity to attend college out of state please take it! I encourage students and people all the time to go away to college. Especially, if you are an African American consider attending an HBCU (Historically Black Colleges and Universities) because that experience will change your life. I was accepted into Columbia College downtown in Chicago. I could've gone there or to any of the local schools in my city but I chose to go away. I am extremely grateful that I made that decision because the education, life-lessons, entrepreneurial mindset and the unconditional love I received from my professors couldn't have been established anywhere else.

To finally be on my own and define who I am was amazing. I wasn't going home every weekend having mommy and daddy wash my clothes, fix my dinner, and check my homework. I was independent and I learned how to do a lot on my own that I would've never felt comfortable doing if I had stayed at home. When I finished college, I was able to say that I did it. That's a feeling no one can ever take away from me.

Finishing college and grad school was a huge accomplishment for me because I've always desired to have de-

31

grees. More than anything, I always wanted an education! Even though I knew it would be hard, I never gave up and I know that what I went to school for was worth it. I know that having an education is better than not having one at all, because no matter what, I will always be educated and I will have my knowledge to fall back on. As I previously stated, I almost didn't graduate on time. My math teacher senior year gave me an F on my final exam. I tried to do everything to change his mind but he was convinced that I didn't know the material. I said, "Is it possible that you miscalculated my grade?"

He said, "No." So you know what I did? I went down to the School of Communications to speak with my advisor. Come to find out I didn't even need the math class. I jumped for joy and said, "Hot diggity dog I didn't even need the darn class." I ran back up the hill and told my math teacher he could keep his F!

He said, "Lauren wait I need to tell you something." I said, "It's too late I already know that I don't need the class so I will be graduating on time after all!"

He said, "Lauren that's what I'm trying to tell you I made a huge mistake when I graded your exam. Your answer sheet fell out and I found it as soon as you left. You passed the exam!" I said, "Are you serious and I began to laugh. I told him thanks for informing me of the error but I'm glad you made a mistake."

He said, "Wait what I don't understand." I said, "You gave me an opportunity to prove to myself how passionate I am about receiving my degree and I just learned that I won't allow anyone or anything to stand in my way. If I encounter a problem I refuse to accept it. I will find a solution and change the outcome especially when it comes to my education."

During slavery, African Americans weren't even allowed to get an education. Our ancestors fought hard for us to be able to read and write. I would be crazy if I deprived myself of the opportunity to increase my knowledge. That's why when the opportunity presented itself for me to attend college out of state I took it. If I were to get laid off from a job, at least I know that I can apply somewhere else because my degree will qualify me. Although finding a job can be hard even with your degree and experience, eventually you'll land something.

I'm willing to sacrifice who I am for what I can become. I don't want to live paycheck-to-paycheck. I don't want to live at home with my parents for the rest of my life. I want to further my education so I can always have something to fall back on no matter what. I want to provide for my parents the same way they did for me. The best way to repay them is by having an education. I want to make sure that I utilize all the values and skills that my parents instilled within me and I can do that by enhancing my knowledge. I want people to speak volumes about my character and when I open my mouth, I want them to say, "Wow Lauren you speak so eloquently."

Some of the things you should start thinking about now are why do I personally want an education? What can I do to receive the best education? And after I obtain an education, what am I going to do with what I've learned? Are you going to start your own business? Will you become a journalist or a pediatrician? The question is how far are you willing to go to further your education so you can have a prosperous future?

You see, the key is to understand that even though you may not have a job, you can create one because of the knowledge you have. P. Diddy was fired from Uptown Records and guess what? Because of the knowledge he obtained in college, he was able to create Bad Boy Records. Yes, he dropped out, but in the end, he returned to Howard University to get his degree.

Another example I love to use is that having an education is like having a suit in your closet. You would rather have a suit and be prepared for an interview than to not have a suit at all. I actually was just conversing with a colleague the other day and he expressed to me how his girlfriend doesn't have a degree. He said he's constantly trying to find her a job but she doesn't qualify for a lot of the job opportunities he finds because they all require a bachelor's degree.

It is so critical to have a degree in this new era. Back in the day, you might have been able to get away with not having a degree. But now almost all jobs require it, even McDonald's. You might be able to get a job as a cashier or a cook. But applying to work as a manager or even an assistant manager without a degree, more than likely won't happen. I've seen people get paid more money when they have a degree. Yes, there are some scenarios when people with a degree may get paid below their value but more than likely they will get a raise. When I worked at Victoria's Secret I was able to receive a raise faster than some of my counter parts because I had a degree. I've also seen people get laid off from jobs that they've been at for over twenty or thirty years because they don't have a degree.

A perfectly good example is my uncle, who is a manager at Blue Cross Blue Shield (BCBS). He recently told me that several people who have worked at his job for over thirty years were laid off because they didn't have a degree. It's extremely sad but it happens every day in corporate America.

I've witnessed what can happen to a person without a degree and I made the decision at an early age that I wouldn't be caught without one. I told myself that I've come too far to let not having a degree stop me from achieving my dreams. I want to be a role model for my peers and for young adults who feel like they have no outlet. I want to be an example of the positive outcomes that can come from going to school. I want you all to know that you shouldn't shortchange yourself; because once you have an education the sky is the limit. You will have the knowledge, the mindset, and the tools you need to start your own business, execute interviews, or come up with creative ideas that will make you marketable!

My dad always tells me you should think of education like Pepsi Cola (it's for the new generation) and like Coca Cola (it's the real thing). Education is the new thing that's in, just like having a new pair of Jordan's.

My experience at Howard wasn't the easiest but I made sure I wasn't going to fail. When you get to college, you need to go meet with your advisors, get to class on time, turn in your assignments, build friendships with your class-mates, join organizations like the debate team, sororities/ fraternities, or band; get to know your professors, look for internships, and manage your time correctly. I know my freshman year, I built a bond with all my professors, classmates, and advisors.

As I previously stated, I've never been savvy in math. My math teacher from freshman year could've given up on me but because I had a great relationship with him, he gave me extra credit work to do, stayed late with me practicing problems, and made sure that I understood the material so I could stop failing the quizzes and tests. My math teacher believed in me even when I didn't believe in myself. That's the type of motivation I needed.

When my sophomore year rolled around, I still was worried about math but I was a little bit better at it. In 2008, I lost a family member that I was extremely close to. My grades, especially my math grade brought my GPA from a 3.7 to a 2.8. I was more than sad. I was depressed all year and especially over the summer. But that next semester, I came back to college with a new mindset. I knew that my cousin would've wanted me to get back on track. I began to think about how much she empowered me to never give up! In 2009, I did extremely well in all my classes, I was going above and beyond in my honors fraternity, Phi Sigma Pi and I was working hard to become a member of Alpha Kappa Alpha Sorority Incorporated (AKA). Even though I went out for AKA in 2008 and I didn't make it I wasn't going to let my past stop me. In 2010, I officially became a member of AKA and that was a glorious day for me because I worked so hard for it. I tried out for Phi Sigma Pi twice because I didn't make that the first time either. Of course, I was angry when I didn't make these organizations the first time but not making it taught me what hard work, passion, humility and strength really are. That's why when the math teacher told me I didn't pass my math final senior year, I wouldn't take no for an answer.

By the time my senior year came around, I was no longer naïve to possibilities that could exist. I knew if I worked hard enough I could create one. My four years in college were all memorable and I learned something new each semester. As I previously stated, those four years made me the strong, passionate, aggressive, and knowledgeable woman I am today! I can't stress enough how important it is to be extremely dedicated to your studies, and to also be involved in extra curriculum activities while you are in college.

I was on a dance team and the speech team. I became apart of an honors fraternity and a sorority. I was in a city club that motivated young students from Chicago to attend Howard University. I also participated in student films and school plays. Getting an education, creating a positive image for myself on campus and attending college was the best decision of my life. I can't say it enough! I absolutely would go back to college in a heartbeat because I had that much fun. I learned so much. The best piece of advice I can give you is to experience it for yourself. That way you can go through life with no regrets.

I want you to start thinking about why you want an education? If your answer is because your parents told you to get one, then you need to reevaluate your response. Of course it's natural for you to want an education because your parents told you they aren't going to settle for mediocrity from you. But the main reason I think you should want an education is to better yourself. Education will allow you to take advantage of any opportunities that come your way. I'm very passionate about the history of African Americans and all ethnicities that have endured racism. It's disgusting that Hitler and the Nazi's discriminated against Jews. When I read about slavery, as well as watch movies and documentaries about slavery, it's sickening that they didn't want blacks to receive an education. Do I have to reiterate how they didn't want blacks to know how to read or write? This is the reason why I would be ashamed of myself if I didn't take advantage of all the educational privileges you can receive today.

Do you know how hard it was for our ancestors and how many of our ancestors fought for us to rise to greatness? That's why when I read on Twitter that a young lady didn't even know who Maya Angelou was, it made my stomach cringe. Her excuse was that they didn't teach about Maya Angelou when she was in school. So what if they didn't. It's your responsibility to do the research and find out who your impactful black leaders are. We know about the latest music. Why shouldn't we know about our black leaders?

Please make sure you think about what our people sacrificed to get us where we are today. Remember that someone marched to get us here, someone cried to get us here, and someone died to get us here. It should be our duty to give something back. Ask yourself who you can educate? Ask yourself what is the value of education to you? Ask yourself if you're not educated, how else will you be successful? Some of the most successful people didn't finish school, like Bill Gates, Sean "P. Diddy" Combs, Steve Jobs, and Kanye West. But I can guarantee you that they have done research and read several books. I promise you, in order to be successful you have to have knowledge. There's no way around it. If you really believe school isn't for you then look into trade school. A trade school is a technical school or a vocational school that is used to teach skills related to a specific job. You can become an electrician, plumber, carpenter and so much more. At least you will have options and you will have a better chance of being successful verses if you don't have an education at all.

Whether you pay money for your education or educate yourself, you want to be well rounded because you have to know how the world works. When you start making six figures, you have to know how to manage your money. Putting it in someone else's hands can be taking a big risk, especially if you don't know how the system works.

I know getting an education can be discouraging because you're not guaranteed a job after graduation. But trust in God's plan for your life, and I promise you that education will come in handy. You want to sell yourself with the most prestigious accolades when you make it to the top. Like I stated earlier, look at P. Diddy. Even as successful as he became, he still went back to Howard University, my alma mater, and received his honorary doctorate degree.

Having an education is important. When you have an education, all you're doing is making yourself more established and more polished. What's wrong with that? A great man said, "You can shackle my hands, you can shackle my feet, and you can throw me in a deep hole to suffer. But it doesn't matter if you do all of that and more. I will always still be free because you can never enslave my mind."

So answer the questions I stated above. Just in case you forgot what they were: Why do I personally want an education? Ask yourself what is the value of education to you? Ask yourself if you're not educated, how else will you be successful? What can I do to receive the best education? And after I obtain an education, what am I going to do with what I've learned? Are you going to start your own business? Will you become a journalist or a pediatrician? How far are you willing to further your education so that you can have a prosperous future? Also, ask yourself do you want to attend school out of state or in state? Why or Why not? Do you want to attend an HBCU or a TWI (Traditionally White Institute)?

Write down your responses and see where your head is when it comes to furthering your education. Doing each exercise at the end of every chapter will enhance your writing skills.

CHAPTER THREE

CAREER

⌒

After I graduated college and graduate school, I wanted to start off in my career right away. I wanted to make a lot of money. I wanted to start on my journey of being successful at a young age.

Unfortunately, it doesn't always end up that way and things don't always go as planned. But just because things turn out differently, that doesn't mean that you have to give up or that your dream won't come true. It's definitely still possible! It only means that you have to remain patient and prayerful no matter how much you want to throw in the towel. Remember, it's only a delay not a denial.

For example, my plan after college was to be a reporter, and then transition to being an anchor. Unfortunately, that didn't happen. Instead, I received a full time job as a manager at a retail store. Then I was accepted to graduate school and I had to let the job go. Of course, I tried to keep the job, and attend school, but they couldn't work around my schedule. Managers have to be able to work on the weekends. I would've had to take a day off on the weekends, which wasn't acceptable especially as a new hire. I had a big decision to make. After speaking with my parents and my family members, I decided that leaving Gillyhicks was the best decision for me.

Why? My education was more important and I didn't want to spend the rest of my life working in a retail store. While I was in grad school, I worked at Victoria's Secret as a sales associate and I interned at ABC 7 news station. After my internship was over and I completed grad school, I was still working at Victoria's Secret but I needed more money.

In 2014, I quit my job at Victoria's Secret and became a full time substitute teacher. Although I didn't end up as a reporter or an anchor, I think God had something better in store for me, which was inspiring the youth. It all makes sense now, but let me rewind and start from the beginning.

In seventh grade, I gave a speech in my communication class. That's when the teacher decided that I had a gift when it came to speaking. She told me that I should deliver the farewell address speech at my eighth grade graduation because she knew I could impact my class. I told my parents the good news and they helped me prepare my speech. When I was practicing, I began to get excited and I really started feeling the words I was using. But it wasn't until I went up on that stage that I really felt my classmates' spirits.

Of course, I was nervous because it was my very first speech. I didn't know how the audience was going to receive me, and when I was practicing at home, I kept messing up. To my surprise though, I couldn't believe how well my speech turned out. Being on that stage at the age of thirteen was the most powerful feeling I've ever felt! I left my heart on that stage, and I was captivated by my classmates' reactions when I finished.

From that moment, I knew that I loved to uplift people. I've been a motivational speaker ever since. I believe that God knew then that I was supposed to be in a role where I gave back to people and students everywhere through inspiration. But you see, I didn't know God's plan for me at the age of thirteen because the motivational speaking just became a hobby for me. I began to speak at elementary schools, high schools, shelters, and at my church with my dad. I was becoming well known in the Chicagoland area but motivational speaking still didn't hit me as something that could be my moneymaker and my career.

Even in college, I majored in Broadcast Journalism and I minored in acting. But you know the funny part? Motivational speaking still found its way back into my life. To be accepted into Phi Sigma Pi National Honor Fraternity, I wrote a speech. For Alpha Kappa Alpha

Sorority Incorporated, I wrote a speech and a motivational rap. People still talk about the speeches and rap that I did in college but I still said to myself, "That's just something I do. Anybody can do it."

It wasn't until this year that God opened up doors for me and showed me that motivational speaking is my gift. I kept asking in January of 2014, "God, why do you have me as a substitute teacher? I didn't go to school for this. I don't receive any salary or benefits, and some of these students are so disrespectful." I was angry with God for a while because I didn't understand why he would bring me this far with two degrees, two organizations, and internships, then put me back at my old high school as a substitute teacher.

I remember one particular day so vividly because I had just pulled up to the school and I broke down crying in the car. "God why me?" I couldn't stop crying but I realized that I had to pull it together because I had no choice but to go to work. I sat there for a minute before I jumped out the car and asked myself, "What could I do to love this job?"

You know what the first thing was that popped into my head? Motivational speaking. I said to myself, "During the last ten or fifteen minutes of class, I'm going to start talking to these kids about bettering themselves. If this is what my reality is, then I'm going to make the best of it."

Although I hated substitute teaching at first, God knew that I would grow to love it because with the substitute teaching I was able to talk to the students about college, scholarships, the value of mentorship, and respect.

No, it wasn't in my job description to discuss these topics but it was in my heart. Here I was subbing in a class full of African American students who felt like no one listened to them, who felt like they weren't going to be successful, who felt like after high school they didn't know what to do next. I knew this because I listened to their conversations among their friends as they poured their hearts out about their doubt and confusion.

Most substitute teachers just read their newspapers, type on their computer, or talk on their cell phone. But not me! I figured out along the way that I had to use my gift to encourage kids in my classroom and around the world. I made it my duty to leave that high school on a great note by impacting my students, helping my students outside of class, and caring about their personal well-being. That's what I'm passionate about and I receive fulfillment in my heart when I know that I'm the reason a young person's life changed.

It is very heart warming when students email, write, and tell me face-to-face how I've empowered their lives. I remember when I went to Chipotle and a student said, "Hi Ms. Ward."

I said, "Oh hi. How are you?"

He told me the scholarship information I gave him really helped and he thanked me for being such a great teacher. As soon as I sat back in the car, I told my mom what the student said. She said, "Lauren that's beautiful." I said, "Thank you mom because that comment really empowered me." There was another time when I ran into a student at Walmart. He was so happy to see me. We had a very good conversation for about ten minutes and he also explained to me how much I influenced his life. The student reminded me about the prayer sessions we would attend in the morning at the high school.

After we would leave the prayer sessions, we would feel inspired, like we were on top of the world. Even though some days me and some of the other students felt like we weren't seeing results, we didn't stop attending those prayer sessions. We kept going back to receive more and more empowerment.

There were so many students who impacted my life as a substitute teacher but I really appreciate one student in particular because she saw me at my lowest points. After class was over I was alone and I broke down about an email I received. The email stated that I was over qualified. The student who I mentioned saw me at my lowest point, heard me crying, so she came back into the classroom. She was there to comfort me. She hugged me and asked me if she could call her dad because she knew he could put me in contact with the right people. I said to myself, "Wow, that's God. These students really care about me. The fact that she didn't judge me for crying but instead embraced me allowed me to realize the bond I was creating with my students."

There were several days when students would get a signed pass by their teacher so they could spend their lunch period or gym period with me. They were interested in college, scholarships, and entrepreneurship so they craved to receive more helpful advice from me. There was another student who had a free period to deliver mail to different classrooms but instead she would ask for a signed pass to pick my brain about scholarships, job opportunities, grants and college. She explained to me that she wanted to be in my presence to receive some positive energy because being in a toxic environment where rumors exist and physical altercations arise is not the scene she wants to be apart of. I told her how I could understand the desire to be in a positive environment. I expressed to her how sometimes I was frustrated by her peer's behavior. She expressed to me how some of them might not appreciate the knowledge I was trying to impart on them but that she was extremely grateful and blessed to have me in her life. I said, "Thank you so much because comments like that really just make my day." She gave me encouragement and at that moment that's exactly what I needed.

49

It's actually really funny because as a substitute teacher the students technically don't belong to you but those students became mine. You couldn't tell me those weren't my students! I prayed for them, I cried with them, I went to see some of them off for prom, I proofread their letters for college and most of all, I loved them unconditionally like they were my own children.

That's why when I speak, I honestly feel like I'm serving a greater purpose to enhance those students' confidence and to let them know that they can be successful in anything they put their mind too.

It took those students to help me realize that God was sending his angels through them to encourage me along my journey. Even though there were some students who were my obstacles—and as young people say, you will always have haters—I didn't let that break me. You will always encounter enemies throughout your lifetime but it's your job to be that rare flower that still blossoms like a butterfly. Some of those students I met were truly heaven-sent and I can't thank God enough for placing them in my life.

Not only did the kids care about me but the staff cared about me too. After school, I would sit in the library for hours speaking with teachers and substitute teachers about life. These women impacted my life and truly encouraged me to keep going no matter how much I wanted to give up on myself. These women poured wisdom, knowledge and love into my life abundantly and I can't thank God enough for allowing them to play prominent roles in my life. I also can't forget one staff member who truly never gave up on me, encouraged me to keep subbing and became one of my closest friends. She saw me at my worst, I saw her at her worst, and we saw one another at our best. We never judged each other all we did was encourage one another.

When I came in there angry, sad, or depressed about not having a job in my career field, this young lady always had some unconditional love and powerful words to send my way. I remember when she reformatted my resume so that I would have a better chance at landing a job in my field. This girl knew her Bible and she was always sharing a Bible verse with me. She told me to keep my head up and she reminded me of how much the kids loved me. She reminded me that I was a great person and that it was important to surround myself with people who want to see me win. She said, "Lauren, I want to see you win."

She began to pray and cry with me. "Lord just please order her steps. Help her to understand that if you brought her out of a difficult situation before, you will do it again." I remember she would tell me about how my name was circulating among the students so quickly because they wanted me as their substitute teacher. I knew her statement to me was the truth too because teachers began to request me. I said to myself, "This can't be real. I'm only a sub." But to those students, I was more than a sub I was their role model.

It really made me cry when the disrespectful students began to behave in my class. I will never forget this freshman student who snuck in my class! I made an announcement that if I caught anyone in my class who didn't belong, I would write them a referral. When I said that, he charged towards the door. Before he walked out I said, "Why did you feel the need to sneak in my class?"

He said, "Because Ms. Ward, I remember you from the first time you wrote me a referral. You told me then I could do better. I remember when I had you for in-school suspension. You could've given up on me but you didn't. You explained to me how I needed to respect my teachers because they can give me information about scholarships and financial aid. You also told me they could put me in contact with people in my career field. I gave you a look as if I would never change my behavior and you could've stopped caring then but you never did. I remember what you said to me, Ms. Ward, and you impacted my life. I apologize for sneaking in your class but I just knew that you were going to do a motivational speech at the end and I couldn't miss that."

I said, "But you would've missed class!" He said it was worth it because at least I know you care. I said, "Sweetie, you can't stay in my class. But if it means that much to you,

I'll let you come back during my SRT class. As long as you get a signed pass from your SRT teacher I'll let you come in my class."

He was elated. "Okay Ms. Ward. I'll see you during study hall."

After my entire class left it resonated with me what the student said and I began to cry. I couldn't believe that I impacted him that much. I couldn't stop thinking about SRT that afternoon because I was thrilled that I would get the opportunity to motivate him again. At the high school I taught at, SRT is a study hall class. Most of the students do their work, but of course you will always have a few students who try to bend the rules. I made sure during my study hall classes that my students were productive and that they left feeling motivated. Most of the students were always excited to receive me as a teacher. Some of the other students were happy, but they knew I was going to make sure they did their work. They knew that when they were with me, they were going to learn something profound about their culture. The students knew my teaching style very well and they became familiar with me. I didn't have to say put your cell phone away anymore or focus on your work because now they did it automatically. I earned the respect that I deserved from my students and it felt good!

One student said, "Ms. Ward several students respect you because you go the extra mile to influence us in a positive way. To be honest no one looks at you as a sub they all respect you as a full blown teacher."

That statement was priceless and it made me feel like I accomplished my purpose at that school. There was no way I was going to let a student leave that room without being encouraged and inspired. I felt like each class period, God gave me a message to deliver. I had to fulfill his will by passing along valuable information.

I have challenged myself to leave behind a legacy! I think what Martin Luther King, Nelson Mandela, Rosa Parks, and several other great leaders did is phenomenal because they impacted lives. I challenge you to ask yourself who have you inspired and what can you do to uplift someone? It's so important to always strive to be a role model because you never know whose watching you. You could have a younger cousin, sister, or brother and you have to set that example for them, so they know how to be successful. You can start by finishing school and then starting your career. Let them know that it's not easy, but anything is possible.

It's necessary that you give anything you're passionate about your all. It's you that will make a difference. It's hard because you may feel like giving up but you have to keep fighting. It's worth it because in the end you will prove to yourself that hard work pays off, and when it's done you will feel so much better. When you complete the task that you worked so hard on, there's no one that can ever take away what you accomplished. I don't care if you feel discouraged. I don't care if you feel like you're not good enough. I don't care if someone told you that you wouldn't amount to anything! You can determine your future. You have the will power to take control of your career. You write the ending to your story. You define how far you will go in anything that you do.

Your obligation should be your career so you can live an abundant life. Whatever career path you choose you should want to be the best at what you do! Nobody knows your story, so how can you allow him or her to tell you what job or career you're supposed to be in? Don't spend your life being miserable because you didn't follow your dreams! I don't want you to have any regrets. How you do that is by following your heart and figuring out what you're most passionate about! If you are having trouble figuring out what you're supposed to be doing then ask yourself these various questions.

When you wake up in the morning what do you think about? Do you think about writing, drawing, or singing? What do you find yourself doing when you have spare time? What could you wake up every day and do for the rest of your life without getting paid?

I know for me, I could wake up everyday and motivate students for the rest of my life through speaking and writing for free. That would truly bring me fulfillment. I could even wake up every day and report on stories in my community to help end the violence and make people aware of what takes place in our neighborhoods. I want young people to know the good and bad that exist in their communities. From my reports they can decide whether they want to be a product of their environment or if they want to change their environment. I can genuinely see myself being a spokesperson for a company or a talk show host for a television station so that I can motivate the world on a global spectrum. The key to the mystery is that once you figure out what you're supposed to be doing, eventually they will have to pay you because you do it so well. Don't worry young people the money will come!

For example, I didn't start off getting paid when I did motivational speaking. But now, I usually get paid for any speaking engagement I do. I started from the bottom with motivational speaking but now I'm at the top because I earned respect from my audience. It feels so good knowing that I worked hard for this title. It's okay to do more than one thing because I don't feel I fall in the category of doing one thing either. But you do have to master your craft or crafts. You need to be focused on one dream at a time and then I promise you everything else will fall into place.

Look at the African American actress KeKe Palmer. She started off as an actress and now she is making history by being the youngest talk show host as well as the first African American to play Cinderella on Broadway. Keke is an actress, singer, musician, talk show host, fashion designer and more. She does more than one thing so it can definitely be done but you have to master one skill at a time. Which is why Keke launched her career through her skill of acting first and it gave birth to all of other dreams like singing, fashion, and hosting positions.

Another thing I want you all to know is that it's okay to dream. It's okay to ask yourself where will I be in five years? For me, in five years I will have my Ph.D., my own place, be successful in my career, traveling the world and probably be married. It's okay to create a vision board. When you do, make this board specific. If you want a BMW don't just say you want a BMW. What color do you want it to be? What year and what model? You know how you take time out to make sure you send the perfect text message or perfect email for a job opportunity? Well take time out to make the perfect vision board for your career.

Don't short-change your future. You owe yourself more than that!

And you know I have to address this issue. There are so many young people who think it's cool to sell product, crack cards, sag their pants, steal, and go to jail, but that mentality will not get them far. Even though they think making "quick money" is cool, if they get caught they have to pay the bail money and they have to pay for a lawyer. That's almost two thousand dollars that they would've spent to get themselves out of that situation. I understand that as a young person you want to make money. I did too. But why compromise your integrity and your character for a few hundred dollars?

A well-respected author said, "We have to teach our generation what it means to be a felon and what it means to get a felony because once it's on your record its permanent. You have to ask yourself in what way are you willing to sacrifice for your dream?" Be creative and put your talents to use. For example, lets say you want to be a musician but you can't afford to buy a drum, right? You know how some musicians began? They began beating on a wash bucket. They were able to make a great sound by using a pen and the bucket. That may sound silly to you but it's all about thinking outside of the box. You may have the supplies you need or you may not but it's all about creating something out of nothing.

It's all about entrepreneurship, young people. I promise you. We have to stop waiting on someone to give us a job and create our own opportunity. Maybe you're good at hair. Open up your own beauty shop or barbershop. Maybe you're the next rapper or singer. Make your basement into your studio so you can come out with an album.

Right now I'm training at a radio station as a fill-in reporter/anchor. I'm extremely blessed and grateful for this opportunity. Even though I'm not getting paid, the experience has been amazing. I'm just humbled and blessed that someone finally gave me a chance. This opportunity with the radio station came from networking so I have a few stories to share with you about the importance of building relationships.

For the past two and a half years I've been working hard by networking. Earlier this year my contacts really paid off when I went to the Black Women Expo with my little sister and I met a young man. My sister spotted him and said, "Lauren, you definitely need to speak with him." I took her advice, introduced myself, and the rest was history.

I started calling him to set up appointments. I would text him to see when we would be able to collaborate on some projects together. I told him that if he needed me I would be available to assist him with anything. Let me tell you how good God is. I ended up running into him again at a local National Association of Black Journalists (NABJ) meeting, and that's when I found out he worked for WVON radio station. WVON is the only black owned and operated radio station in Chicago, Illinois. I was honored and blessed to even be speaking with him because WVON is one of the highly respected radio stations throughout the country.

He told me about how he came in as an intern at the radio station but he proved himself and he was able to move up to the fulltime news reporter spot. I said, "Man, that is a blessing!" He explained to me how he would come in early as an intern, stay late, and volunteer for events the station hosted. He also told me how he started recording himself doing the traffic, news and weather. He would send the samples to the hiring manager and the hiring manager kept stating how he was getting better and better. The manager didn't ask him to do that but he took the initiative to do it. He said that he started claiming he would be the next news reporter and that's exactly what happened! Someone ended up quitting and he was there to fill the spot. The manager didn't even question whether he could do the job or not because he had proven his talent. This young man is a great example of how you need to work hard, be dedicated and passionate about getting your foot in the door even when you are an intern. After he moved up from an intern to an employee, his boss was interested in hiring some fill in reporters, so the full time reporters could take days off.

Next thing I knew, I received a text message from the reporter stating that he had recommended my name. Like I tell my students all the time, it's not always what you know but who you know. His manager called me, left a voicemail, and stated that he wanted me to come in for an interview. I couldn't stop crying when I listened to the voicemail his boss left because I was so grateful that the reporter recommended me.

I went in for the interview and to my surprise, the manager of the station had already watched my newsreel and gone over my resume. He asked me to tell him some stuff about me that he didn't already know. I began to tell him about my internship experience. He stopped me right there and said, "Well you have great internship experience, but what about your work experience?"

I said, "I haven't had my first job opportunity but I know I have the education, skill set, and mindset to execute any task that is given to me."

His face became puzzled. I could tell that he doubted if he should bring me on board.

At that moment, I put my head down. When I lifted my head back up, I had tears in my eyes. I said, "Sir, with all due respect, I will never be able to become successful if no one gives me a chance. Someone had to give you a chance and I feel that I'm qualified enough to be given an opportunity to prove myself. I know I only have internship experience, but isn't that the point of an internship, to intern and then work your way up to the job opportunity? I've been turned down so many times because I haven't had my first job. But I promise you I can do this! As I stated earlier, I have the education, experience, and mindset to be your next fill-in reporter. All I ask is that you believe in me?"

He said, "Ms. Ward, I can feel your spirit and I can see the passion in your eyes. So from what you just said, I'm going to take a chance on you."

I began to cry hysterically. The manager said, "Ms. Ward, are you okay?"

I said, "You don't understand how much this means to me because for so long I've been waiting for someone to take a chance on me. The fact that you finally did speaks volumes about your character." I told him he wouldn't regret hiring me and I would prove to him how great I could be. Now I'm training with the morning reporter. I'm learning how to do news, traffic, and weather on the radio. All I could say was, "To God be the glory." It has been such a great experience and I'm learning so much. The manager told me if I can prove myself, I'll be speaking on the radio very soon so that's what I'm aiming for.

One of the most important things that the morning reporter is teaching me is about juggling different hats, something that he does very well. He's a reporter and a rapper and that is how he's making his money, doing what he loves.

At first I had trouble cutting off my personality when I did the news, weather, and traffic on the radio but he helped me to be more conversational. Now I can do my motivational speaking and my reporting smoothly without struggling through it. It's an amazing feeling to be doing what I love.

In 2014, I was very depressed but WVON helped me gain my confidence back and to go full throttle after my dreams. The most thrilling part of it all was getting one of the most popular Chicago local artists on the radio station.

One day I was on YouTube and my students were always talking about two young ladies named Tink and Dreezy. I took it upon myself to find out who those young ladies were. Their talent impressed me. I instantly connected with Tink because not only does she rap, but she sings too. I'm a very sentimental, soft, and loving person so I loved all her music. "Bonnie & Clyde," "Treat Me Like Somebody," and "Lullaby." I fell in love with her music and I said to myself, "I have to get in contact with this girl somehow, someway!" I started looking for an email on her through Twitter and Google. I don't remember exactly how I did it but, I found her manager's email on a website.

I emailed her, praying to get a response but I didn't receive one. This is where persistence kicks in because I thought to myself, "She's probably really busy." So I continuously emailed the manager once a week and finally received a response. Tink's manager was impressed with how polite, humble, and established I was. I told her I wanted to be a mentor for Tink and I would love to have our radio personality interview her on our station. Her manager agreed to it, gave me Tink's contact information, and the next thing I knew, I was on the phone with Tink.

She was very sweet, and the show was "off the chain", as young people say. People were tweeting about the show, posting questions on Facebook, and liking our pictures on Instagram. The show was a success and my manager was like, "Girl, you could be the next fill-in reporter and a producer."

I was so proud of myself at that moment because I worked really hard to get that contact and I did it all on my own. I wasn't asked to book Tink. I took the initiative to do it. I was beginning to prove myself and people were noticing how determined I was. I knew that I deserved to be a permanent member at WVON and I wasn't going to leave until they saw everything that I could bring to the table. I started thinking in my head, "The next person I'm going to book is KeKe Palmer." My mind began to expand and I began to think bigger and bigger.

Young people, when you get an idea don't sit on it. Please run with it because you never know where that opportunity can take you. In one day I built up my reputation and earned the respect from my colleagues that I yearned for and had always deserved. That's why I'm so grateful for the reporter who ended up becoming my friend because he recommended me to be a part of that radio station. Between his recommendations, his manager bringing me on board, and the WVON family welcoming me, I blossomed. I started off in a cocoon and became a butterfly. Even though I wasn't sure about this career path of being a reporter anymore, there were signs that journalism, communications, and motivational speaking was where I belonged.

Another great example of networking is how I was hired at Rainbow Push Coalition two days after producing my first news segment on air at WVON. It was unbelievable! In June of 2014, I emailed the president of ABC-7. I didn't receive a response, but I didn't take it personal because I knew he was extremely busy. Then I received a text from my god mom who works at ABC-7 News saying that her boss, the president of ABC-7 News, invited me to come to the Rainbow Push Convention because he wanted to meet me in person. I was super excited. I texted her back and said of course I will be there.

I went to the convention and I met so many great people. It was a pleasure to meet the President of ABC-7 News in person and we set up an appointment for me to come into his downtown office. I was elated and blessed that he even asked me to come to his office. After we were done speaking, I went back into the convention to sit down and that's when I spotted Rev. Jesse Jackson Sr. As soon as I saw Rev. Jesse Jackson Sr. walk on stage, I said to myself, "I have to meet him." When he came off the stage my god mom introduced me and she told him I was Yogi Ward's daughter. He said, "Oh I know Yogi. He's a fantastic man and a great entrepreneur."

I said, "Thank you," and then I started to speak with him about job opportunities.

He said, "Sweetie, I have to run. Please speak with Josef Mase."

I thought to myself, "Who is Josef Mase?" I didn't see a man standing close by so I felt defeated at that point because I couldn't find him.

The next day at WVON, I was telling my co-worker how great the Rainbow Push Convention was and I told her how the only sad part for me was that I couldn't find Josef Mase. She said, "Josef Mase?"

I replied, "Yeah, Josef Mase!"

She replied, "Lauren, I have his cell phone number and his email. I'll call him for you."

I said, "Wait … what … are you serious?"

He didn't pick up the first time she called, but when I was leaving the room she yelled for me to come back because he was on the phone. I raced back and I spoke with him. He gave me his contact information when I asked for it and told me to call him after the convention.

I followed up with him the day after the convention was over but he was still busy. So I let a few days go by and then I called back again. He answered and I asked him if he had time to speak. He said, "Yes. You have about five minutes. Go ahead." I did my elevator speech, which includes my background at college and what I was currently doing.

After that, he said, "I want to put you in contact with our educational director and senior advisor for Rainbow Push."

I said, "Wow. Thank you so much," and he took down my phone number.

Now young people this is when it gets critical! Although he had taken down my contact information, I know how busy people can be. I didn't want him to forget about giving my contact information to his employee so I went on Google and found her email address myself and to my surprise, she was a soror. A soror is a woman that is in the same sorority as me. I was jovial when I found out this woman was an AKA.

I emailed her right away but the email returned to me because it was not in service anymore. This is why I say it's so important to network, especially at events, because I texted my friend that I met at the Rainbow Push Convention. I asked her if she had the woman's updated email address and she said yes and gave it to me. I emailed the new address right away and this time it went through. I ended up falling asleep but when I woke up in the morning, I had an email from her saying, "Hi Soror Lauren. I look forward to meeting you, and can you stop by Rainbow Push at six p.m. so we can talk?"

I emailed her back and said, "Of course I can."

After work, I went home, put on my best dress and

shoes, and headed back to the city. When I pulled up I saw another soror walking in the headquarters and she asked me if I was there for the community meeting. I replied no and told her I was just there to meet with the educational director who is also the senior advisor for Rainbow Push. Low and behold, I ended up being at the community meeting with other members but I still had no clue why I was sitting there in the meeting.

Another reverend gave me a yellow folder and said, "These are for the instructors." I'm thinking in my head, "Instructor? I wasn't told that I was going to be an instructor." After we did our introductions, the administration team then told me that they wanted to bring me on board as the Multi-Media Journalist Instructor. I had the biggest smile on my face and I was like, "No way! How did I come in for a meeting and leave with a job?" I couldn't stop tearing up and smiling. I looked up and said, "Look at God."

The woman told me the position was temporary but after my introduction, she said, "We will be sure to find you a permanent position here or at another prestigious company."

I said, "Thank you so much." I then mentioned to the director that earlier I heard them discussing a meeting they were having at church the next day to end gun violence. I asked the reverend if she needed someone to cover the story. She said, "Wow Lauren, you're on top of it. Yes, I would love for you to cover the story."

I said to myself, "Lauren you're good girl and it's amazing that you're taking the initiative."

That night I told the morning reporter I would be coming to the station in the morning to get the equipment because I had a story to cover and report on. He said, "Okay Lauren. Wow that sounds good to me."

The next day I went in, collected my materials, and headed to the church. I recorded the audio, took pictures, and interviewed people. I wrote the story that night and the next day I was on the air reporting the story. My manager and the CEO of WVON heard my story and they were impressed. That was one of the proudest days I had this summer and it's one I'll never forget because once again I took the initiative.

Everyone tuned in that day to hear my first newscast on air. My family, close friends, and my WVON family all supported me by listening to me on the air because they knew that was my dream. So not only do I thank the WVON family for believing in me but I have to thank my parents, my family, and friends because they helped me to accept God's plan for me. I was so discouraged these past two and a half years but 2014 really gave me my hope back. I went from working jobs that weren't in my field to working jobs that are in my field. I was able to attend meetings with the CEO of WVON who is a powerful and intelligent African American woman. I had the privilege to work with Rev. Jesse Jackson Sr. who is an influential man that marched with Dr. Martin Luther King, Jr. I also had the opportunity to meet the Jackie Robinson West Little League Team and Mo'ne Davis. If that is not a blessing and an honor then I don't know what is.

My little sister asked me to attend New Faith Baptist Church with her. She began speaking to me about how I should accept teaching and motivational speaking as my career. I said, "No Jett, I'm supposed to be a reporter and anchor. I'm supposed to be a spokesperson for a television network or brand. I'm supposed to be a famous actress, and be the next Oprah or Iyanla."

She said, "That could very well be true, but you're not going to get there on your plan. The only way you can get there is on God's plan."

At that moment I said, "You know what? You're right. Let me go back to the drawing board and figure out how I can understand God's plan." That's when I said to myself what about your book? You started on your book called "The 6-Step Plan," but you never finished it.

Do you know that I ended up going to a girlfriend's going-away party (she was moving to New York) and giving a motivational speech? I told my friend how proud of her I was, how she should follow her dreams, and I discussed how I decided to finish writing my book. Who would've known that this would've turned into another networking opportunity?

After my speech was over, her uncle came to me and said, "So you're writing a book?"

I said, "Why, yes I am."

He said, "My wife and I publish books."

I said, "Oh my God, are you serious?"

He said, "You speak so well. Here's my card and a free copy of Mary Dee's new book that my wife and I published."

I was grateful that he saw something in my speech and that's why I always say it's so important to put your best foot forward in any situation because you never know who is observing you. I was honored that he gave me a free copy of the book and I made sure to keep in contact with him. It is so important to follow up with your contacts, young people. Whenever you receive someone's contact information, make sure you follow up. If you really want to stand out you can send a hand written thank you card. It's good to thank a person through emails but sending a handwritten thank you card really makes a difference.

Now, young people not only am I training and interning at WVON as a fill in reporter but I also was at Rainbow Push as a Multi Media Journalist Instructor. I wrote this book and I began conducting teen writing workshops that showcased how writing can be a positive outlet for young people. These opportunities all came from networking but it would've never happened if I had not followed up with my contacts. From me following up, I have a couple that wants to publish my book.

God was already setting me up for success and I didn't even know it. Let me tell you how God took it a step further after I met Mr. and Mrs. Woods.

I was on the phone with Mr. Woods discussing the process of publishing my book and he told me that they could put it on Amazon, E-Books, and several other places that would benefit me. He said they could do all of that for an amount well over a thousand dollars. Instantly my heart sank and it was beating fast. I couldn't afford that amount.

I explained to Mr. Woods my financial situation and he asked if I could pay in increments. But I knew with me being an intern/ trainee at the radio station and with me not being at Rainbow Push yet paying to get my book published wasn't even an option for me. Mr. Woods said, "Lauren, you know what? Send me your resume and some of the links to your video." I sent him everything right away and I was praying that he saw something in me.

Him and his wife called me back and said, "Lauren, we wanted to inform you of some new information."

I was very nervous! I'm thinking in my head like, "Oh my God, I must have done something wrong."

Mr. Woods said, "Lauren, after reviewing your resume and after me and my wife watched your videos on You-Tube, we want to publish your book for free!"

Instantly I began crying and at this point, I was hysterical I said, "Look at God." One of my favorite songs by Jekalyn Carr is "Greater Is Coming," and that's exactly how I felt. I was emotional and I kept thanking this God-sent couple. They said, "Lauren, we believe in your dreams. We know you're going to become a well-known speaker, author, journalist, and talk show host. We just want to be a part of making that dream come true for you."

I couldn't believe that someone had believed in me again and had recognized all the hard work I've been putting in for years. I was humbled and grateful. I just thanked them for taking a chance on me and I told them I wouldn't disappoint them. Then Mr. Woods even took it a step further and contacted a woman who wants to put my book in the Chicago Public Library. She wants to pay me to do a teen writing workshop, motivate the students, and discuss my book. She even said she might have me to do a book tour.

When I spoke with her on the phone, she said, "Ms. Lauren, I have to say as a sister, as a mother, as a Christian, and as a black woman I was highly impressed with your videos on YouTube and your resume. I'm extremely proud of you!"

When she said that it made me tear up because I couldn't believe how many people I was impacting. Her response and the fact that she even wanted to pay me to speak to her children and do the teen writing workshops made me think, "Is this really happening?" The teen writing workshop was a success. I discussed how to write a great essay. I discussed my book, entrepreneurship skills, how to create a business plan, how to create a vision board and I had them break out to do writing exercises with one another. Do you know that the woman in charge of the program was so impressed that she recommended me to do this same program at more libraries throughout Chicago?

My family said, "See, we told you God's plan is much bigger than your plans." So after all of this, I thought God was done, right? Nope. God said, "Let me really just break this girl down so I can show her what I've been prepping her for all this time."

I did a motivational speech and my famous motivational rap at an Elementary School. All my family and friends couldn't make it that day but it was so comforting to have my little sister there to support me. As I walked onto the stage, I said, "I'm going to give this audience my all." I was a bit nervous because I'm used to speaking to an African American crowd and this was my first time speaking to a large crowd that was predominantly Hispanic and Caucasian, with only a few blacks. I didn't know how they were going to receive my message but I still was confident and enthusiastic. I made sure everything I said related to issues they would be facing in sixth through eighth grade.

When I was finished with my speech, I had a question-and-answer segment. One student asked me, "What do you do if you have a friend that wants to commit suicide?"

I answered that question to the best of my ability but even then, it still didn't hit me on how my responses were affecting the children. But when I was completely done with my speech and I walked away to go gather my things, I turned around and had a line full of students standing there to speak with me. My little sister couldn't even get to me fast enough because the kids were jumping up and down to speak with me.

The first student said, "Ms. Ward I just want to say you have inspired me," and then she began to cry. When she began to cry it made me emotional because I didn't know how much my speech impacted her life. The next student after her said similar words and she also began to cry.

At that moment I began to realize that this is really my gift that God blessed me with. How could I have ever doubted my calling? I became so emotional because these kids were saying how I affected them, but they affected me too. They made me feel that my motivational speaking was worthwhile and that I should keep going because I have a powerful message to share. I asked the other students what they were standing in line for and they said they just wanted a hug. I collected several of their emails and gave them encouraging words to keep them going. But the very last student in line blew me away.

She asked for my autograph, which really made me tear up because no one had ever asked for that before.

Even though I didn't know what to write, she said, "That's okay. Just write anything." Then she said that her friend had been thinking about committing suicide and she wanted me to speak with her. The fact that she trusted me with that type of information put the icing on the cake.

That's when I began to encourage myself by saying, "Lauren follow your heart and trust your instinct. I know you're not making any money right now but the pay off will be more than you imagined because you're changing lives and saving lives."

She took me upstairs to the student's classroom and I spoke with her friend, who had cut herself and was thinking about committing suicide. The young lady didn't want to open up at first but when I took her away from everyone and I had her one-on-one, she fell into my arms like putty. The school was already aware that this problem existed with the young lady so they were relieved that she was speaking to me about her problems. I have my little cousin Brandon (who I also call my little brother) to thank for that. He helped me to become a great communicator when it comes to speaking to teenagers or children. If the school had been unaware it is always good to report the issue so that the young person who is suffering can receive help but luckily they were in the process of getting her the assistance she needed.

All that young lady needed was someone to listen, someone to care, and someone to show her genuine affection. See young people, this is how I want your career to feel. I want it to be like a radiant vibration that you can't control because you think about it in your sleep and when you wake up in the morning. Like the coffee commercial says, "The best part of waking up is Folgers in your cup." The best part of waking up for you should be fulfilling your dream. That really doesn't feel like work because you fall deeper in love with it every time you do it.

It should be a magical feeling that excites you and you shouldn't let anyone take that feeling away from you. The moment you do, you'll stop dreaming. That's how I know motivational speaking is definitely apart of my career plans because uplifting young people is something I could do everyday.

Another way you will know when you found your niche is when people compliment you all the time about it and they make you feel like what you do is a skill. For example when I traveled to New Orleans to attend my line sister's wedding, I was reminded of what my true calling might be. I was in the car with my boyfriend, my two line sisters and their boyfriends. One of my line sisters boyfriend, asked me if I'd had speech lessons before? I said, "No, but I'm looking into taking some because I'm a speaker and a reporter, so it's important that I speak well."

He said, "That's what I'm talking about—for you to have never had a speech coach, you speak very well. I've been listening to you speak since we got in the car, and you speak so well, Lauren."

I said, "Wow, thank you."

He said, "You're so welcome. Seriously, you're really good because most people use 'um', 'uh', and other filler words but you don't."

I said, "I didn't notice, but thank you so much for the compliment." That was another green flag that made me think to myself, "Here is someone who just met me and he really loves my voice and the way I speak."

Don't take your talent for granted, young ladies and young men. I almost did. If you have a gift, accept it and use it to the best of your ability.

As I stated earlier my co-worker from Victoria's Secret is one of the people that influenced me to finish this book. I was humbled when I started naming my 6-Step Plan and my co-worker said, "Wait, let me get a pen and paper because I want to write this down for my daughter." That made me feel special. Writing this book has really made me feel like I make a difference in the lives of young people and adults. The proof was in the putting when I was speaking to my little brother and he said, "Wait, don't tell me. I know your 6-Step Plan by heart because I wrote it down after you left."

I said, "Wow, really? You did? What is it?" He told me what each step was and he got every one right! That made me so happy and of course you know I cried because now I knew that he was listening to his preachy and talkative big sister.

These experiences are what make me tell young people to search deep within and find out what your special gift is that God has given you. Don't hesitate, because you don't want to put off for tomorrow what you can do today. Make it happen right now. Don't let age be a factor. Whether you're ten, thirteen, fifteen, seventeen or older, just keep God first, get an education, and figure out how you can make money for the rest of your life by being your own boss. In 2014, God really made a lot of my dreams come to the surface and he gave me an opportunity to start living.

In 2013, I attended the NABJ convention with intent of landing a job. I met celebrities, news directors, and several other prominent people in hopes of being hired, but I was disappointed because nothing came from those connections. However, I did come close to landing a job with ESPN, but for whatever reason it did not work out. I was extremely hard on myself because I was angry that I made so many connections and still didn't have a job.

Then 2014 rolled around and I began to think back to all the connections I made the previous year. I said to myself, "You know what, Lauren? What if God was planting seeds in 2013? Several of the people who attended last year will be at the convention again this year."

As far as celebrities, I met Tyrese, Jenifer Lewis, and Derek Luke at the 2013 convention. But one celebrity who I was most honored to meet was T. D. Jakes. Jenifer Lewis was very personable, and Derek Luke was nice too. You could tell Tyrese was tired but when I stood next to him I made him smile by singing "I'm a Capricorn, these are the signs of love making." I know Tyrese is a Capricorn like me, so that's why I chose that song. He began to laugh and it turned out to be a great picture.

For some reason it was very hard for me to get next to T. D. Jakes but I was not giving up until I spoke to him. From the moment he walked on stage I kept saying to myself, "Lauren you have to speak with him." When he came off the stage I tried to speak with him but his security team was too tight. His manager began to say no more pictures and no more autographs. I felt defeated. But then the spirit of God came through me and said, "Girl don't give up. You're so close."

I began to follow the security team and they dipped off into a back room. I started sweating while I was entering the room because I knew it wouldn't be long before security knew I didn't belong. The door slammed shut and it was one of those awkward moments because everybody started looking at me.

I said, "Hey, how y'all doing?" One of the security guards moved closer to me and I knew he was probably about to grab me and kick me out the room. As soon as I felt him about to grab my arm I spoke up and said, "Reverend T. D. Jakes, it's just an honor to be standing in your presence. I know I'm not supposed to be back here but I had to speak with you. I'm a journalist and an upcoming motivational speaker in the Chicagoland area. I would love to give you my business card so that we can keep in contact."

He said, "Thank you so much for your beautiful compliments." He then accepted my business card and handed it to one of his team members. He put both of his hands out and said, "Let me pray for you, my sister." I began to cry because his prayer was beyond amazing! As he was praying for me, I kept saying to myself, "God please let me reconnect with this man again, whether it's in person or through email. He's my inspiration."

After he prayed with me he said, "I have to go, sweetheart, but I know that God has nothing but greatness in store for you."

You see young people, even though I didn't get a job that year that experience with T. D. Jakes was priceless. Later on, I had to remind myself of the people I met and the connections I made. I had to give myself a pat on the back because looking back on my experience I did network really well. I had been focusing on how much money I spent to get down there and I was angry that I didn't get a job. But I had to realize that my experience was not a waste of time. Sometimes you may think that God is moving slowly but in all actuality he's setting everything up so it will be on time. I learned from that experience that even if nothing comes from the opportunities, just appreciate the fact that you were able to be in that environment.

I can't wait to attend the NABJ convention again this year and I'm praying a job opportunity comes from it. But if it doesn't, I know the experience will once again be phenomenal. I'm keeping a positive attitude and looking forward to making those connections. Always maintain an optimistic outlook on everything.

Even though I didn't have much money to attend the NABJ convention again this year, that's the point of a savings account and networking. My savings really came in handy and I told my little sister she had to come with me this year. She knew we both didn't have the money to go but I told her I would take care of it and that's exactly what I did. I started asking my mentors, friends of my family and people from my church for donations. Because of my work ethic, character and people wanting to see me succeed I was able to raise a substantial amount of money for my little sister and me. Young people, I can't stress enough how important it is to network because people will reward you for your hard work especially if they know you personally. For example, when I interned at ABC-7 News my god mom bought me a laptop and in 2014 she paid for my plane ticket to the NABJ convention. My god mom adopted me as her god baby because of the relationship she has with my dad. My dad is the king of networking and he made sure I knew the importance of networking so now I am constantly talking to people. That's why it is so important to be respectful, and listen because when you burn bridges with people they don't want to work with you anymore.

The teacher you disrespected or the friend that you were rude to could've helped you to get your first job, internship or write a letter of recommendation for you. I also want to remind you that it is okay to use social media to post pictures of your family and friends as long as it is appropriate. It is best to stay away from pictures that symbolize sex, profanity, fights, drinking alcohol and drugs. To capture the right audience you should use your social media to advance your career. I'm not saying you can't have fun with your social media but you definitely have to use your judgment with what you post. You don't want a situation where the things you posted on your social media from childhood are now haunting you when it comes to applying for job opportunities. For example, I am always on Facebook, Twitter, Instagram and LinkedIn networking. I messaged a prestigious man on LinkedIn who worked for The Chicago Defender, Ebony Magazine and Flowers Communications. To my surprise he messaged me back and it's been history ever since then. I was extremely proud of myself because that is a connection I received for my sister and me. He gave us great advice and he has been very helpful in our career search. Even when I'm at WVON and Rainbow Push Coalition I'm constantly networking.

I met with two CEO's within two months from networking! I met with the CEO of WVON and the CEO of Johnson Publishing Company, which is the home of Ebony and Jet magazine. Young people, networking has been going extremely well for me and I know God is about to open several doors because of it. I forgot to mention that not only did I meet the young man from WVON at the Black Women's Expo but I met Lisa Raye as well. Do you know that Lisa Raye asked me to mentor her daughter? I couldn't believe it! We are still working on a date to make it happen but once again it came from networking.

I met Kym Whitley at the Black Women Expo as well and I messaged her on Facebook and do you know she responded back? Although, she couldn't help me at the time she told me to stay in contact with her. She said when she has more time she will help me or pass my information along to someone who can assist me. All of these blessings came from networking so don't be shy young people. Most recently, I was the Mistress of Ceremony for the Howard University Gala and after the event was over

I was networking as usual. Do you know a Senator's wife approached me and asked me for my contact information because she wanted to send me a free copy of her book? Then she told me I was brilliant and that I should consider going to divinity school. I was shocked and humbled all at the same time. She told me to stay connected with her because she said she would do anything in her power to make sure I succeed. I said, "Wow, networking can really take you far." That's why I am encouraging you to attend conventions, workshops and seminars so that you can meet new people. You will never get anywhere keeping the same circle of friends. You have to meet new people in order to make it!

The next time you get ready to look up the show times for a movie I want you to also look up the next conference or convention that will be in town. Find professional settings like workshops or seminars that you can be apart of! Join your church choir, join a book club, or look into volunteering with different organizations. You should start thinking right now of how you can get involved so that you can start networking.

Age is nothing but a number so I know you can make it happen. My boyfriend and I are 25 and 26. Age or money could've held us back but we decided at a young age that we wanted to travel. Our families always compliment us because we have traveled a lot especially in 2014, and we're proud to say that we've been out of the country. I remember when I went to Paris, Italy, and London in high school. I've always loved traveling. It's in my blood! I knew as a kid that I deserved to live a life of prosperity. This year alone, my boyfriend and I went to D.C. for my little sister's graduation, as well as Cancun and Miami for vacation. We went to New Orleans for my line sister's wedding (and let me just say that New Orleans is a super fun place). Next, my little sister and I are going to Boston for the NABJ convention. Then in October, we're going to the Dominican Republic for my older sister's thirtieth birthday.

At the age of twenty-five, I feel I owe it to myself to travel. So with my savings account, my last paychecks from substitute teaching, and my boyfriend's income, we made it happen. I also used my credit card but we will discuss how to use a credit card in chapter four. I was ready to live my life that year. Even though I wasn't making a substantial amount of money from work, I decided to step out on faith and start traveling.

Go after what you're passionate about because you'll have a long lasting career that you will love. You have to believe that you will be successful. You don't need anyone else's approval so validate yourself! It's really just about knowing you. I really love to travel. I genuinely love meeting new people. I know that God will allow me to travel, and network as long as I continue to work hard and I believe in my dreams. If you don't remember anything from this chapter young people just remember that I said to network, network, and oh yeah NETWORK!

In this exercise, I want you to answer these questions on your sheet of paper. I have also included the questions that were asked earlier on in the chapter. The first question is asking yourself who will be on your team on your journey to success? When you wake up in the morning what do you think about? For example, do you think about writing, drawing, or singing? What do you find yourself doing with your spare time? What could you wake up every day and do for the rest of your life without getting paid?

Who supports your dream right now? Do you know what your purpose in life is? Do you have an idea of what you want your career to be? If you could travel, where would you go? Last question, and you probably know what this one is why is networking so important? Answer these questions, write them down, and work towards making them a reality.

CHAPTER FOUR

YOUR OWN PLACE

I can't stress enough how nice it is to have your own place in college or after college. In order to have your own place, you have to earn a nice amount of money. It's as simple as that. You can start by getting a job and putting some of your money you get from working into a savings account! Have your parents take you to the bank so you can open up a savings account. I don't care if you have to start off at Walmart, Target, Forever 21, or Pizza Hut—just get a job when your in high school so you can start saving money for college and one day have your own place. You're a teenager; so working in retail or fast food isn't going to kill you. Trust me. I worked at Carson's, JC Penney, and Express so that I could make money and start a savings account.

Of course, it depends on your situation. Some people may not have time to work while they're in college so that's why you should start saving your money in high school. For example, if you receive a check for $100 then you can start your savings account by putting away $20. A great long-term goal would be to save $20 from every $100 that you make. If you don't have a job, then budget the allowance you receive from your parents. You can spend some, but save the rest. But if you can work in college, or in high school, then save that money for a rainy day because you will need it. I know it may be tempting to buy the newest pair of Jordan's or splurge on clothes in high school, but in college your mentality and your priorities must change. Instead of itching to buy the newest clothes and shoes you should start thinking about saving your money to rent your first apartment, pay off your first year's rent comfortably, pay off your student loans if you have them or take vacations.

Trust me, there are more valuable things that you'll want to do with your money, as you get older. The worst feeling is to go away for college or live on campus in-state and get a taste of freedom, then have to come back home. I live with my parents now and I'm twenty-five, which is okay because I'm working and saving money. But of course my plan is to move out as soon as possible; especially once my career is set in stone. Now granted, I'm an only child so my parents aren't pushing me out the door, which is a blessing. I'm challenging myself to work harder, because I'm ready to give back to my parents!

My parents are amazing. They've sacrificed so much for me and they have been so supportive of my dreams. I'm ready to do everything and more for them because they deserve it. That's why I just want to state again if things don't go the way you planned directly after college, it's okay as long as you're trying. This is when you can start thinking about creating your own opportunities, like I did. I wasn't able to find work so I started writing my book, working on my website, hosting the teen writing workshops at different libraries and building my brand. I had a lot of time on my hands so I began to use my time wisely.

If you do happen to move back in with your parents, just make sure you're productive, saving your money, and doing something to contribute to the household. I know when I get paid I give my mom money for the groceries, I give my dad money for my bills, and I try to take my parents out to eat. I really prioritize my money. That's what you should do if you want to secure your future. I really am striving to be successful before thirty. Of course everyone has different definitions of what success is, but mine is pretty simple.

Being successful to me is my 6-step plan! It's understanding where God is in my life, my education, my career, having my own place, marriage, and kids. I want to be independent, and having all of this would make me feel like I grew up and became the woman my parents raised me to be.

I take my savings account very seriously. It's comforting to know that if I ever have an emergency or when I finally do end up in my career and I'm making good money, I'll have a savings account to always fall back on.

It's okay to admire someone. But the way young people idolize Nicki Minaj, the latest shoes, or a cell phone can mislead you and make you forget about the important things you should focus on at your age. I believe that you should idolize having your own place or buying your first car on your own, because once you make this step; you can really call yourself an adult. Making a move like that proves how responsible you are. When you're in control of what takes place at your household and you pay the bills, you can really feel good that you're the one who made all of this happen. Even if you have a guilty pleasure and you buy your first authentic leather jacket, it is an excellent feeling because you will feel accomplished. You can say to yourself I worked hard to purchase that jacket.

Personally, I desire my own place not only because I owe it to myself but also I owe it to my parents. I want to show them that they raised me well and that I learned from the example they set forth.

I also want my own place because I want privacy and freedom. I want to invite my friends and boyfriend over for movie night or just to listen to music, as we play cards. Not that my parents won't allow me to have company but there are strict rules if I choose to invite anyone over. I went away for college so while I was there I had privacy and freedom. I didn't have my parents to remind me to do my homework and wash my clothes. I was responsible for all my actions but being back home is different because your parents sometimes forget that you are an adult. A lot of times parents want you to stay their baby forever so its hard for them to see you as an adult. Once you get your own place that will help change their perception of you and they will accept you as being a responsible adult. Having your own place is the coolest thing; trust me.

The new thing that's not cool, is young people having five or six kids and not attending college. That won't get you far at all. It's different if you're a mom with a plan and you're actually trying to accomplish your goals. But to just get comfortable and keep having baby after baby with no plan is not smart.

Focus on your dreams and your goals, and get your own place so you can set the rules for how things go in your household. Having your own place is the equivalent of never having to depend on anyone taking care of you again. As an adult, this is something you're definitely aiming for because you control where your money is going. Whether it's for bills or to go out, you determine what you spend your money on because now you're independent.

Take for example my older cousin, who I call my older sister. She's doing extremely well and I'm so proud of her. She attended Howard University and graduated in 2007. Then she attended DePaul University Law School, passed the bar the first time and became a lawyer at the age of twenty-five. She moved out of my aunt's house and into an apartment at the age of twenty-six. She recently bought a home and she did all of this before the age of thirty—she's only twenty-nine right now!

She's on my 6-step plan and is doing very well. She keeps God first in her life, she has an education, her career, her own place, and she's looking forward to marriage and kids. She's living her dream and she is actually doing what she went to school for. She is very happy and she is making a substantial amount of money for a 29-year-old woman. Oh, and guess what young people? Because of her new promotion, this young twenty-nine-year-old will be making six figures very soon. You know the emoji that does the handclap? If I could put it in this book I would because she is a black woman who's excelling in life. She's an excellent role model. I admire her so much and she gives me inspiration to keep working hard so I can achieve that one day.

I've worked very hard to have that type of success before the age of thirty because I don't want to be forty or fifty before I get married and have kids. I want to have a lot of my adventures while I'm younger because I know when you get older there are certain things that you may not be able to do.

My family always told me growing up that your twenties are supposed to be the years used for partying, hanging out, and traveling. After thirty you need to really start settling down and you should pretty much be set with a plan on where you want to go in life. Many of my counterparts are young and successful, including my older sister. So I want to strive for the same thing. I mean, why can't I have it? I've done everything right and according to my 6-step plan it's just a matter of time before it turns out the way I want it. You should never compare yourself to others because what God has for them is for them and what God has for you is for you but you can always admire someone's work ethic. I admire her and she motivates me to keep working hard until I achieve success.

Another thing that I want to reiterate about the savings account is that in your twenties it really does come in handy. Remember earlier in the book I told you that my boyfriend and me went to Miami, Cancun, and New Orleans? One of my friends was like, "Dang Lauren, how are you traveling but you're not working right now?" I told her it was because of my savings account, my boyfriend's income, my last paychecks from substitute teaching, and my credit card. She said, "Wow Lauren, You really are a great saver." I saved up so much money that when I would spend money on my credit card I paid it right back with my substitute teaching check or with the money in my savings account. What you don't want to do is max out a credit card. I have a few friends who have done that.

Never spend more on your credit card than you can pay back. You want to build up your credit and make sure you can always pay your bills on time. Always remember no credit is bad credit (creditors look negatively at a person who has no credit at all). Also, if you pay your bills late or you don't pay them at all, that can give you bad credit as well.

Oh and if you're discussing moving in with your significant other—because a lot of young people are living with their significant other—then have a serious conversation with that person. You should ask your significant other what their credit score is. You want your credit score to be seven hundred or above because 720 and up is considered excellent credit. 719 to 680 is good credit. 679 to 620 is an average credit score, so as you can see if you're in the mid six hundreds, that's fair. But anything 619 and below is considered poor or bad credit. So if your credit score is between 619 to 580 that is a poor credit score. If your credit score is 579 to 500 that's a bad credit score and anything below 500 is considered a really poor credit score. Meaning when you try to buy your dream house or even apply for loans you will be denied. I just want to inform you ladies and gentleman of what my parents have told me, just in case you do consider moving in with your significant other. However, I suggest that you wait. If you do decide to move in together anyway at least you know what questions to ask.

In my opinion, it's always best to get your own place first, just to experience living on your own. When I had my own place, let me just say it was everything I prayed for. I had my own place when I was in college and I had my own place when I was in grad school. It was more than amazing. It felt like a piece of heaven. I came and left as I pleased. I had privacy. I had my own rules and I felt accomplished. In my freshman year of college I had a roommate and it was a great experience living with her. Thank God to because I have heard some horror stories about roommates.

I lived in a dorm room called the "QUAD" and it was a lot of fun. There were hallway parties, we played IT in the dark, we had slumber parties and there were several college parties that I went to. By the way, if you attend any college parties or parties in general just be sure to always watch your drink, don't go anywhere alone and be very observant of your surroundings. But nonetheless I had my own place for my sophomore, junior and senior year. My sophomore year I lived in Meridian "M-Dot" and I lived alone. Oh my God, living on my own and living in Meridian was so much fun. It was a co-ed dorm so there were a lot of pranks that the girls played on the boys, including myself. I definitely participated in some of the shenanigans.

My junior and senior year I stayed in the West Towers. I had joint apartments for both years, but having my own room and my own door made me feel like I was on my own. Junior year I pledged AKA so I couldn't do as much but freshman, sophomore and senior year I went on spring break. Freshman year was the best because my roommate, two friends and I went to Miami. I can't stress enough how fun college was. Not only do you get to be on your own, but also you can travel, take road trips and go to homecomings. Especially Howard's homecomings! We truly have one of the best. People who graduated in the 70's and 80's still come back.

I know I got a little off topic young people but bare with me I had a flashback of college but moving right along I had an apartment in grad school and it was really nice too. I decorated it. I started grocery shopping and cooking more. My friends and boyfriend would spend a night. There were a few nights when my friends came over to play board games, cards and "IT" on the jungle gym after hours but for the most part I was responsible.

The last thing I want to say to you in this chapter is please start saving your money right now. Whether you are in high school, or college it can really benefit your future. You will appreciate the sacrifices you made in the long run. I know it will be hard but trust me it's worth it.

In this exercise, answer these questions and get an idea of what your thoughts are. Do you want your own place? Are you okay with "shacking up"? Why or why not? What can you do now to start working on your apartment, condo, townhouse, or home? If you do plan on moving in with your significant other do you know his or her credit score?

CHAPTER FIVE

MARRIAGE

∽

This step is one step I think every young girl or woman thinks about. But I always say just make sure you're ready. Of course it's natural to want to hurry and get to this step but you have to allow life to run its course. For example, if you want to run track, it's always good to stretch and practice beforehand. That's how you should look at marriage. There are steps and precautions you need to take before you decide on this step. You should aim to start off as friends, then girlfriend/boyfriend, then fiancé/fiancée, and then husband/wife. There are levels to everything in life. Enjoy each level with your significant other as you make your way to paradise.

I remember when I first met my boyfriend at the Taste of Chicago in 2008. He was with his boys and I was with my girls. Of course, my girls and me were playing the game that I'm sure everyone has played, which is who can get the most numbers. The night was young, we were looking good or "fly" as the young people say, and I needed one more number to win. I spotted a group of guys and I told my friends I was going to make the light-skinned guy my final number. I approached him and attempted to talk to him. But my speech began to slur.

A tall, caramel-skinned boy walking up with a red cap on his head caught my attention. He had a turkey leg in his hand. I said to myself, "He's the one." I walked away from the light-skinned guy, walked right up to the caramel-skinned guy and said, "Hey sweet thang. What's your name?"

He instantly began to laugh and he said, "My name is Tyshaun."

I said, "That's a catchy name. Why don't you let me holla at you real quick and get those digits?"

By this time, he was laughing hysterically and I even began to laugh. I realized that my approach was working. I was imitating how a guy makes a pass at a young lady, and it ended up working. He gave me his phone number and I said, "If I get a chance, I'll call you." I walked away and could hear him laughing as a friend of his said, "Shawty was bad though," meaning that I was a good-looking young lady.

As I ran back up to my friends, I said, "I got the last number and you guys said if I picked the finest one I would win the numbers game." They all put their heads down, then lifted their heads back up again and said, "You're right. You did get the finest one, so you won." I was so excited. I told my friends to take notes next time on how to win. I waited two weeks before I called Ty and when I did, we had the best conversation.

We began to communicate on a weekly basis. Even when I returned to school in the fall as a sophomore, we still communicated consistently. He also helped me to deal with the loss of my older cousin that year. In spring of 2009 we began to communicate daily. We would talk in the morning on the phone, text through the afternoon, and talk all night long on the phone. When I came home for the summer, I immediately wanted to start a relationship with him since we established such a great friendship but he wasn't ready.

We remained friends for the whole summer. Even though our feelings were beginning to grow, we still didn't change the status of our title. It wasn't until I was leaving to return back to Howard as a junior that Ty realized that he was about to lose out on one of the best things in his life.

I remember telling my girlfriends, if he doesn't make it official I'm going to stop talking to him. I told my girls he was playing too many games, but to my surprise, he had an agenda all along.

The same night I was going off about him, he called

me and we ended up going to the lakefront. We were in the car watching the stars and the night was very peaceful. It just felt magical. He turned the music down, grabbed my hand, and he told me he had fallen in love with me. I began to smile and I started tearing up. Then he popped the question for me to be his girlfriend.

Of course, I declined the offer, playing hard to get. But two weeks after I returned back to school, I reconsidered. We officially became boyfriend and girlfriend on August 22, 2009. I can honestly say that summer was the best summer I ever had because I met my other half. We've been inseparable ever since then and even though having a long distance relationship was hard, we never let that break us apart. Ty is my best friend and I am extremely grateful that God placed him in my life.

If anything, the long distance made our relationship stronger because we both knew what we wanted was to be with each other. I was faithful to Ty and he was faithful to me. We both had experienced the single life, and at that point in our lives we were ready to settle down. Since we were both on the same page there was never any infidelity.

Of course, we missed one another, but thank God for Skype and Oovoo. I honestly have to say that I'm extremely grateful that Ty taught me how to have patience. If we hadn't established a friendship first I don't think we would know how to handle the good times and the bad.

Since we're best friends, we learned how important it is to support one another, communicate with one another, and value each other's thoughts or opinions. We learned how to let our guard down and just love one another unconditionally. When we endure bad times like being low on funds we encourage one another and we appreciate that we have each other, so we don't have to struggle alone.

That's why I was elated when the title changed from friends to girlfriend/boyfriend. It was easy to make that transition because without knowing it, we were already building an unbreakable foundation. We were planting the seeds that grew into an endless friendship and then into an equally yoked relationship.

August 22nd of 2014, will be five years that we've been a couple. I know you're probably saying to yourself, "When are we going to get married?" We're not rushing into anything because we aren't financially stable. What I mean by financially stable is we need to be making a substantial amount of money in our respective careers.

Ty recently did get hired at an IT company and he receives a salary and benefits. He was blessed to find a job opportunity in his field but he has to grow with the company, in order to make a substantial salary. I know within a year or two he should be able to get his own place, but right now he's focusing on eliminating some bills. Also, when Ty does purchase his own place not only does he want to be able to take care of himself he wants to be able to care of me. He takes note of everything my parents do for me and as a man he wants to provide for me the way my parents do. Ty has a great relationship with both of my parents, but of course he strives to mirror what my dad does for me. Ty wants to make sure that when he ask me to move in with him that he can take care of both us especially if I haven't found a job yet. Which brings me to my next point.

At least Ty gets a consistent paycheck but me on the other hand, I don't have a consistent paycheck coming in or benefits. The radio station is great, but as I stated earlier, I'm not getting paid yet. And Rainbow Push is only for the summer; it's for six weeks. If I get a permanent job at the radio station or Rainbow Push, now we're talking. I would receive a salary and benefits. But until then, I can't make any drastic moves. I refuse to be living in debt when I marry my significant other. I don't want us to always focus on bills and be stressed out about money.

In order to take this step called marriage you need your own place because to me marriage is sacred. I wouldn't want to get married and still be living at home with my parents. If we are husband and wife, I want us to have our own place and be able to take care of ourselves.

When I get married I want my husband and I to travel. I want us to come home and have the luxury of doing what we want. We can't do that if we're still living at home with our parents. It would be impossible. Also as I mentioned earlier, I don't want my husband and I arguing about little things that can ruin our marriage. I want my husband and I to be able to go out to eat, go shopping, or travel without worrying about money.

I remember when my boyfriend and I were both working minimum wage jobs. The thought came in our heads to move in together and get married but we were both like, "Nope, it's not going to work." I want us to be making fifty thousand dollars or more—even six figures—so that money will not be an issue. I'm not implying that we both have to make six figures in order to get married but we both definitely want to make a significant amount in order to be comfortable. That's what my boyfriend and I strive for. I feel like that's the best option because we want to stay married forever and we're willing to do what it takes to have the best marriage and secure our future. I know some of you might feel like there are a lot of people in your generation that are getting married, but go at your own pace.

Set the rules for your own relationship and don't compare your relationship to anyone else's. You don't know what goes on in their household and you don't have the right to judge anyone. If you have friends or family and it seems like things are working out for them, be happy for them and understand that is their blessing. God will bless you with your own opportunity, you just have to be patient.

If you desire a relationship, a nice house, a nice car, or your own place, you will receive that as long as you continue to work hard and you understand that your blessing is being directly designed for you.

Take me for example. I waited for two-and-a-half years for opportunities like WVON and Rainbow Push. I'm beyond grateful that I finally received them, but I had to wait and remain loyal to God. I still have a lot of work to do to get to where I want to be, but hey it's a start and that's what I kept asking God for.

Don't focus on what others are doing, what others are saying, or who others are "kicking" it with. Just focus on what you have to do and cherish what you already have. Of course I want to get married, but I know that right now isn't a good time for my boyfriend or me. I know that if we want to have a successful marriage, we at least need half of our ducks in a row. What I mean by that is we need a structured foundation. We can't think that after we get married we're going to be happy with no money and still living at home with our parents. That's an epic failure. I want the best for us, just like my parents do and his parents want that too.

My parents set the standards high by getting married first and then moving in together. That's the example I want to follow. My parents dated for thirteen years and they have been married for twenty-eight years. If you add all of that up then it's a total of forty-one years they have been together. No marriage is perfect because no human being is perfect but growing up in their household showed me what true love is. I remember staying up late watching them step downstairs in the family room off Luther Vandross or Earth, Wind & Fire. As they would sneak in a kiss or a soft "I love you," I would laugh. Of course as a kid when you see your parents do mushy stuff it makes you uncomfortable, so I always laughed. Sometimes late at night I would sneak downstairs to watch my parents step but I always got caught. That's a memory I will always cherish. I remember the boutique of flowers my dad would buy for my mom, the chocolates, teddy bears and random road trips they would go on.

Witnessing a foundation of love growing right in front of your eyes, as a child, is one of the most beautiful sights you can see. I want that magical and amazing experience with my significant other that my parents share. I know some people like to "shack up" but my parents showed me that sometimes the wait is worth it. Why, because you appreciate it a lot more and waiting builds up the anticipation.

The wait will make you work much harder. You won't rest until you have your own place and you won't rest until you are married to your better half. I know some people move in together because they need a roommate, it can help to produce more income, or their simply in love which is fine. But just to do it with no purpose other than the fact that "everybody else is doing it" is not a good idea. You want to at least try to save something special for when the two of you get married because living together, especially when you're not engaged, can slow down the process of you getting a proposal. Or it can take the fun out of what it's supposed to feel like when you do get married. I know a high school couple that just graduated from Thornwood high school and they were planning on moving in together but over the summer they broke up. I'm not saying you can't marry your high school sweet heart but I'm just saying don't rush because you have plenty of time to spend the rest of your life with your significant other.

When you get married, you want it to be one of the most exhilarating and most amazing feelings you've ever felt in the world. Don't ruin it by doing it just because you think it's what you're supposed to do after you graduate high school or when you get older. If you want to take that step, then do it because you want to. Don't do anything because society makes it seem like you need to rush into it. Do things according to how your relationship is going. For example, if your boyfriend proposes, you become his fiancée, and now the two of you are discussing moving in together, that's different. Now the two of you have a plan. The plan is to get a place, get married and continue to move forward together. That's why I said if you are going to live together just make sure you have a plan. Get yourself together first financially before you try to take care of someone else.

Another thing to keep in mind about marriage and moving in together is that you become one. There issues like bills, credit and problems all become yours too, so make sure you're ready to take on that responsibility.

It's not just about you anymore. It's about the two of you and the two of you will be looked at as one. Don't get me wrong; I can't wait for that day to come for me and my boyfriend to get married. But until then, it's about getting this money! I'm 25 and he's 26 so we still have time. We have to strive to get into our careers and get our own places so that we can make it to the next step, which is marriage. I'm willing to put in the work now and I know he is too. If I were to get a job opportunity in a different state this would be the perfect time for him or me to go for it. We don't have any major obligations keeping us here in Chicago so the sky is the limit. We want to continue to work hard in our twenties so we can get married, travel as husband/wife and live comfortably because we plan to be financially stabled. Our motto is work hard and play hard, in this order.

In this exercise ask yourself these questions. Am I okay with getting married as a teenager or in my early twenties? Am I okay with living together with my significant other before we get married? Have I asked my partner what he or she thinks about marriage? Am I comfortable with us having two different places and living apart until he proposes? Lastly, ask yourself what do you want and what does society say you need to do? Answer these questions and get an idea of where your mindset is, as well as your significant other's mindset.

CHAPTER SIX

KIDS

I know I already stated that you shouldn't rush into marriage. But you really shouldn't rush into having kids. Doing that can truly alter some of your plans if you don't have the support you need. Some people do have support from their family and close friends, but that is not the case for everyone!

I was at a meeting earlier this week and I knew my co-worker wasn't herself. I asked her what was wrong and she told me that her daughter was pregnant. She was devastated and hurt by her daughter's actions. Her daughter hadn't finished school, nor was the couple married. She also told me that she prayed that the guy would be true to his word and stick around through the pregnancy.

At that moment, I knew she needed encouragement! Instead of saying, "Girl your daughter is doomed. Babies ruin everything," I gave her a positive perspective. I told her, "Your daughter will still be successful no matter what because she has you for a mom, and that's a blessing in itself. She will finish school. She will get married, and we will remain positive that the guy sticks by her side."

You could tell she was sad and disappointed but it's moments like that where you encourage anyone who is hurting instead of discouraging them. She ended up smiling and I was just happy that I was able to be there for her in that moment. This is why I want to be clear in my message. Having children as a teenager isn't always a scarlet letter, but it can be a heavy load on you and your loved ones.

Of course you can still be successful, but the question is do you have that support and are you ready to make sacrifices for your child? To be honest with you, even with support, things can still be difficult. I think if you can wait to bring a child into this world you should. This is just my opinion, but I have spoken with a lot of young mothers and they always say they love their children but if they had waited they could've secured their future a little more for themselves and their child.

Believe me, I know when you meet that special someone the fireworks go off. You feel like you can't live without that person. You'll absolutely die if that person doesn't call you tonight, and you feel like nobody can tell you about your man or your woman. Trust me, I understand. I feel the same way about my man. But as much as I love him, I know we're not ready for a child. We can't give a baby the best childhood and everything that a child deserves. We don't have the financial stability yet.

Growing up, I had an amazing childhood. I was just discussing with my cousins who I call my sisters how we used to have all the toys, how we traveled to Disney World seven years in a row, and how we had nice clothes. I lived in a nice neighborhood, had a nice house, and went to a good school.

If I were to have a child right now, I can't even do half of that because I am not financially stable. My parents enrolled me in ice-skating, gymnastics, ballet, tap, and jazz classes. They also enrolled me in karate. I am extremely grateful that as a child I was involved in a lot so I want my child to have the same opportunities. As a woman who wants to be a great mom, I want to give my child the world because my parents gave me the world. I didn't have to want for a lot of things because my parents worked hard to provide everything I needed. I yearn to demonstrate that type of love and stability that they gave me. I wouldn't be able to settle for anything less because I had the best.

I have so much respect for the women who are single mothers and who have to drop out of school just to take care of their children. But nine times out of ten, if the mother had more support she wouldn't have to do that. In my opinion, a mom who will do that is definitely a great mom because she is sacrificing her education for her baby. But at the same time, you shouldn't have to put your dreams on hold. I think every woman and man should fulfill his or her destiny in life. You should focus on yourself first and then take on the responsibility of another life when you have yourself together. Having a baby is a blessing, but I know personally I want to give my child the world and I can't do that if I don't have a good job.

You even have to ask yourself are you ready to not be selfish? Are you ready to be selfless for your baby? I realized at a young age that when you have a baby it's not about you anymore. As a mom you really have to give your all to your baby because they run the show. If you want to go out, or you just want a night off from all the responsibility, nine times out of ten you will need to let a babysitter or family member know in advance. I know if I were a mom, I wouldn't want to impose on anyone at the last minute. So as far as last minute things occurring, unless it was an emergency I would always want to be prepared.

In my opinion, I know it would be hard to just pick up and move if you have children. For example, I stated that I am striving to be a well-known motivational speaker and a journalist right? Well, say for instance I get hired in a smaller market for a journalism job, the news directors aren't going to give me a month or longer to relocate. I would have to leave that week and start getting set up that weekend to be on the air as soon as possible. If I had a child, I wouldn't be able to pick up and go as quickly because I would have to think about what is best for him or her.

Nowadays you can't leave your child with just anyone. You have to know who you can leave the child with. You have to know if your child will be safe from sexual or verbal abuse. Will your child be fed healthy food or unhealthy foods? Will your child be watching appropriate programs on television or inappropriate programs? These are all things you have to think about.

If you're in high school and you have a baby, it's not that you can't still be successful. It's just that you have to work a lot harder than the average person to make sure you do well in all your classes and graduate. Because usually after the baby is born the mother has to take time off from work or school to recuperate.

From the moment I visited the Howard University campus in D.C., where my older sister attended, I knew that was the school for me. But I knew, if I became pregnant as a high school student I would have to attend college in state. Even though more than anything I want to be married one day and have children the reality is I would never want to separate my family. If I were a mother I would have to alter my plans unless my family is willing to move out there with me. But I didn't have a job in college so I would've more than likely had to stay home. Don't get me wrong there are some great universities in Chicago but I knew that Howard was where I belonged so marriage and kids couldn't be my focus in high school.

I was in love with this one guy in high school too before I met Ty and I thought we were going to be together forever. It didn't work out between the two of us because my goal was to attend college and he had no interest to receive a higher education. He tried to convince me to attend school in state and he wasn't supportive. Can you imagine what would've happened if I had a baby with him? I know that I wouldn't be where I am now because my mindset would've been focused on my child and him. That's why I want to reiterate young people to always focus on your dreams first and if there is someone in your circle that doesn't support that dream then separate yourself. I yearned to go away to college so I wasn't going to let anyone stand in my way.

Of course, I want kids and I wouldn't mind having them with my current boyfriend. But once again, we need to be financially stable and have our own place before we bring a baby into this world. It's bad enough being married and not having money. You imagine what it's like being married, living paycheck-to-paycheck, and having a baby. That's no fun at all. That's why I said don't rush because you have plenty of time to have kids. The best way to bring them into this world is after you're married, you're financially stable, and you've had time to enjoy your life.

You want to have time alone with your significant other after you get married. Enjoy those first few years together. Go on vacations with just you and him. Go out to eat at the spur of the moment. Watch movies, cuddle up, and have no distractions. That's what you need to aim for. Remember I stated in the previous chapter how much fun that can be with just the two of you. Everyone wants to have that perfect little family and you will have that one day. I just suggest that you take care of you first and let everything else fall in place. That way, you're happy, your husband is happy and your kids will be too because you will be able to give them the world.

As a matter of fact let me tell you a true story about this woman I met in Los Angeles. I felt bad for her because she said she was miserable and she felt like her life was over. This woman told me she had several kids, she wasn't married, and she didn't graduate from college. When I tried to cut in to encourage her she cut me off and said, "All my kids have different dad's and I live paycheck-to-paycheck. I have had several failed relationships with my family, friends and colleagues." I said, "Why?" She said, "Because of my spiteful ways." I actually began to chuckle a little bit because I couldn't believe how proud she was about her spiteful ways. At this point I couldn't take her seriously but when she reiterated her situation that's when I knew she was serious.

Unfortunately, because of her financial situation she can't do half of the things that a mother would love to do for her children. She wants to send them to better schools, live in a nicer neighborhood, buy them cars, and give them the type of lifestyle they deserve to live. But she can't because she doesn't live that lifestyle herself.

How can you demonstrate to your child what they should have or what they should do if you haven't obtained it? For example, if you dropped out of high school and you don't attend college your child may not be receptive to you pushing them to go. Another example is if a child grew up in an abusive household. I would hope they wouldn't grow up abusing others but sometimes children go based off of what they see.

It would be different if this woman had a positive mindset and a positive outlook on life. But she can't display that to her children because she is always negative and miserable. I remember one year she told me she was going to adopt children and I was really happy for her. But then she told me she was only going to adopt the children for the money. She also told me if she had finished school, married her significant other, and waited to have her children, then she would be much happier. She has stated that she wishes her life had been different. But instead of her owning up to her own mistakes, she blames everyone for her inadequacies.

The reason why I am schooling you lovely ladies and wonderful young men is because I don't want you to have regrets or be miserable! I don't want to see you have a life that you feel was never your own. You deserve to live a life of happiness, prosperity, peace, and hope. You deserve to pamper yourself and do things the way you want to before your life becomes about someone else. This woman didn't love herself, so she thought having a baby would change that. But it didn't. Since she didn't love herself, that draining energy remains in her spirit.

You know how it is when someone walks in the room and you can just feel that negative energy? That's the type of energy you want to avoid.

This book was created for you to focus on getting yourself together first. Make irrelevant people and drama non-existent. If you don't entertain it, then it won't be able to live in your consciousness. Don't allow anyone to steal your joy and you can remain happy by taking care of yourself first. The way you treat yourself is how you show other people how to treat you. Don't put anyone before yourself when it comes to your relationship with God, your education or your career.

Young people, it's about self-preservation. If you and I are falling off a bridge, I'm going to try to help you—but

I'm going to have to help myself first. You see what I'm saying? Don't shortchange yourself by always putting others in front of you. Of course you want to help others its second nature for me. That's why I was so adamant about creating this book because I want to see young people succeed, especially African Americans because our race has endured so much as a whole. But the reason why I'm able to be in a position to give back is because I made sure that everything with me was taken care of first!

Growing up, it was very hard for me to focus on just doing for myself because I wanted to do so much for other people. But once I realized that Lauren is number one and that I have to do what makes Lauren happy, that's when things started changing for me. I started reading my Bible more, attending church more (whether I was by myself or not), writing my book, preparing for my workshops, focusing more on my motivational speaking and on my career. I started tuning everyone else out who couldn't add value to my life and I focused on the people who could add value to it.

Sometimes you have to love people from a distance and let some relationships go. Misery loves company and if you surround yourself with negative people it will begin to affect you. If you have anyone in your circle that attracts negative energy, run away from him or her as far as you can because they will try to make you out to be the bad guy so they can be the victims. As much as I wanted to help that woman in L.A., I just couldn't. It's difficult to take on someone else's problems especially when you have problems of your own.

Don't allow yourself to be anyone's tragedy. You have to know your worth and be confident with who you are. As I stated in previous chapters, if someone doesn't have your best interest at heart, the best thing to do is move on because it is only destroying your manifestation. In order to be a great mom, a great dad, a phenomenal young woman, or a phenomenal young man, you have to build character and strength. I always used to say that when I pass away, I want to leave behind a powerful legacy. I want people to remember me as being strong, respectful, passionate, inspirational, kind, and a person who displayed unconditional love.

One of those characteristics that I realized early on that I had to work on was strength. Even though I have faced a lot of obstacles, when it comes to relationships with people, I want to hold on sometimes. I had to realize that you can't hold onto every relationship that you have. Some people are in your life for a reason, some for a season, and some for a lifetime. Trust me, the people that are there for a lifetime are the people you need to focus on and give them their roses while they're here. My little sister always told me to focus on the people who praise you and cherish you because more than likely they will be the ones to stick around for a lifetime. She's the one who reminded me to give people their roses while they're here. That's why I cherish my relationship with my little sister so much because she truly embodies what a best friend, sister, and cousin really are. We've been by each other's side since birth and we hold one another down no matter what. I don't ever have to worry about her judging me, or posting crazy things on social media about our friendship because the bond we share is unbreakable.

There is a reason why I call her my little sister because she has always admired me the way I admire my older sister. My little sister looks at me as her role model and I strive to make her proud. That's why I am doing my best to follow this 6-step plan because I know she is watching the moves I make. That's my baby! I inspire her and she inspires me everyday. She and I don't go around being spiteful to people when we let relationships go instead we love that person from a distance because life is too short to hold a grudge.

It takes up too much energy so don't focus on the people who are only there for a season. All you can do is pray for them. If you try to do more, you'll only exhaust yourself.

I hope you can understand why it is so important to have good people in your circle so that when your children do come along they can be surrounded by love and support. You don't want to dig a deep hole in your life that you can't get out of. You never want to be in a position where you don't have anything to fall back on!

Just to reiterate if you have God in your life, if you have an education, and if you have a career, then you'll always be able to stand on your own two feet. Even if you lose your job, you'll still be able to overcome that obstacle. You will have your degrees to back you up, and you will have God in your life so all things are possible through Christ. Who knows? God may give you the wisdom to start your own business if that is what he wants you to do.

Live your life with no regrets, young people. Strive to be the best person you can be every day. If you want to be a great mom one day then write that down but make sure before you become a mom you are prepared. I told you that I strive for many different things, like being a successful businesswoman, being a great mom, and being a leader in my community. I know that with my 6-step plan I can achieve that.

For our very last exercise I want you to ask yourself why you want to have kids? If your answer is because it's the thing to do in our generation, then I am so happy you read this book. Your response shouldn't be that straightforward. It should be well thought out and much more specific. I want you to ask yourself how old you would like to be when you have your first child? Ask yourself what are some of the things you want to provide for your first child when he or she is born? Do you want to provide a nice house, be married, nice clothes and send them to great schools? What are some of your prominent desires you want for your child? Then ask yourself this question: can I provide all those important things right now? If you already have children then ask yourself what can I do to enhance my child's or children lives? Ask yourself what does it take to be a great mom or a great dad?

CHAPTER SEVEN

THE JOURNEY CONTINUES

∽∽∽

I wrote this book because I knew there were young people and maybe even some adults that were searching for guidance. I remember having a conversation with one of my friends who told me to accept my gift! I kept asking her, "Why me? I've never thought about being a minister! I've never thought about doing motivational speaking as my sole career instead of journalism or communications."

She said, "Lauren, anyone who has been called to touch people and preach the word of God should be beyond grateful. Stop fighting it, girl. Go forth to deliver God's message."

Ever since then, I've been living out my dream by touching every individual that I can. I am so blessed to have friends like her who believed in my dream and me.

She gave me that extra push and even though I became emotional, I needed to hear that because it gave me my reassurance back.

Everyone has a story. Even though mine wasn't traditional, with landing a career directly after college, I thank God for all the obstacles and for taking me through the back door. He makes me work so hard to achieve my dreams. And you know what? I appreciate it a lot more now. If I can be the biggest cheerleader for a child, a teenager or a young adult, I will be.

Even though I came from a two-parent home, I know everyone isn't fortunate enough to have both of their parents in the household or to even have their parents at all. I want to let every child, teenager, or young adult know that you aren't alone. Young people, whoever that person is in your life that would do anything for you, cherish them. I still remember how supportive my parents were when I decided to write this book. They were there with me every step of the way. My dad came with me to the library to sit down with the publishers and my mom looked over the contract. I'm just blessed to have them in my life and I know I couldn't have written this book without them. I also know that I couldn't have written this book without my students in the District 227 area because as much as they stated that I influenced them, they impacted my life as well. That's why I included the following email messages that they wrote me in 2014.

Hey Ms. Ward. Please excuse the extremely late response. I watched all your videos on YouTube; I just didn't provide the immediate feedback I should have. You're a very amazing woman and person as a whole and you're exactly what this world needs more of. I'm sure if there were more people like you our adolescent group would be more scholastically inclined to be on the same yacht you reside on.

⚜

I just watched both of your speeches. Keeping your eyes on the prize and never give up on your dreams. You're so amazing in so many ways. I thank God for placing you in my life because you never know who you run across in life because people come and go in life, but it's a true blessing when people like you are around. You just blessed my spirit and future with the powerful words from your speech; God says that life and death are in the power of the tongue so when you're speaking positively things upon my life, you're pushing me to move forward in life. May God just pour and lay his blessings upon you and your family and friends or anybody that is affected by you. Enjoy your weekend and all the blessings that God has in store for you :)

⚜

You're an inspiration to me; if I could I would talk to you about everything, like literally everything that's happened to me. Thank you for motivating me to step into an unfamiliar zone.

⚜

Hi Ms. Ward,

Thank you for referring me to Ms. Middleton. She gave me a lot of information that helped me learn about the classes I will take and programs I would need to be in for physical therapy. I really appreciate your help and it's beautiful what you do to assist young people with following their dreams.

⚜

Hello, Ms. Ward,

I greatly appreciate your concern for my education and job-seeking opportunities. I have not yet looked at your videos but I am sure they are thrilling & educational, as was your speech in my 5th Period Human Anatomy class on Friday, April 11, 2014. I plan on checking out those scholarship opportunities that you sent me the links too, and I will be submitting a FAFSA soon enough. I also admire your oration skills, as it deals with the younger generation. I rarely come across substitute teachers, or teachers in general, that take an interest in their students' lives. The younger generation needs more people like you. The elaborate speech you gave really spoke out to me. I am impressed with your education, & the fact that you come from Howard University, as my uncle is an alumni from there and is currently pursuing employment in psychology. As mentioned before & to reiterate, I appreciate your concern for my development as a person. Thank you for your time & concern.

⚜

Can you please be my mentor? I mean, I can have more than one right? I love you, Ms. Ward. I aspire to be like you; beautiful on the outside and inside. You're the most giving person I know. STAY BEAUTIFUL!

Even when I had a rough day with some of the kids who were disobedient, one student wrote this:

Hey Ms. Ward I was just checking in on you to see if you were okay and to let you know not to let the kids at south get into your head because "lions never lose sleep over the opinions of sheep!"

These are some of the emails I received from students and all of these compliments made me feel special! These students poured their hearts out to me throughout the school year in 2014 and it made me realize that God put me on this earth to inspire other people, to make them feel good about themselves. That feeling is truly priceless when you know you changed someone's life. Even though the substitute teaching wasn't paying me a lot of money, I walked away every day feeling like a million bucks because there was a student who said I impacted their life.

Two thousand and fourteen was definitely my breakthrough year and it took two-and-a-half years for me to understand that. But God knew my purpose. He was preparing me for my greatness! Now that he put me in the right circle, I've been networking, learning and making connections.

I still remember on August 16th of 2014, when God had three angels speak to me. I called them angels because all three of them touched my spirit. All three of them knew who I was but I had no clue who they were. The first angel said, "Lauren Ward I remember watching you on television when you were doing a motivational speech for the kids, you were powerful! Ms. Lady you changed my life." The second angel came up to me a few hours later and said, "Hi I'm Alex. I follow you on instagram and I love when you post pictures, quotes and videos because you are always inspirational."

The third angel was at a play I attended that night and I was on my way to the bathroom when a young lady shouted my name. She said, "Lauren Ward I remember you! It is so good to see you again. From the moment I met you at U of I your spirit, personality and humility touched my heart. May I have a flyer to your event and your contact information?" I gave her all my information and the smile on her face was breath-taking. I couldn't believe that in one day God reassured me of why it is so important that I fulfill my destiny. I didn't know how many people I impacted through my speaking, through my social media and by just being Lauren. I was truly humbled that day and I was grateful that God had each of these angels to approach me. Even though I didn't know them they knew me and they left a mark on my heart that I will always cherish. After that experience I know my calling is definitely to keep impacting lives.

Whether I become a motivational speaker, teacher, minister, talk show host, actress, bestselling author or journalist I trust God's plan. I can be one of those things or all of them. I can only say look out world because here comes Lauren Christina Ward, the woman who believes you can overcome any obstacle as long as you keep your eye on the prize and never give up on your dreams. I will rise to greatness to fulfill my destiny!

"Pay attention to the signs in life because when you feel like giving up that's when your next blessing will present itself!"

—Lauren C. Ward

The End

About the Publisher

Let us bring your story to life! With Life to Legacy, we offer the following publishing services: manuscript development, editing, transcription services, ghostwriting, cover design, copyright services, ISBN assignment, worldwide distribution, and eBooks.

Throughout the entire production process, you maintain control over your project. We are here to serve you. Even if you have no manuscript at all, we can ghostwrite your story for you from audio recordings or legible handwritten documents.

We also specialize in family history books, so you can leave a written legacy for your children, grandchildren, and others. You put your story in our hands, and we'll bring it to literary life! We have several publishing packages to meet all your publishing needs.

Call us at: 877-267-7477, or you can also send e-mail to: Life2Legacybooks@att.net. Please visit our Web site: www.Life2Legacy.com